A Serenade of Madness

(murmurings from a manic muse)

A collection of poetry, songs, and prose
written by:
Angelique M. Gentry

ISBN: 979-8-218-53507-0

First paperback edition date, October 2024

Book design by www.fromthebreathofdaydreams.com

Artwork created in Adobe Firefly by Angelique

Published by
www.fromthebreathofdaydreams.com

Printed and distributed by Ingram Spark

Angelique M. Gentry

A Serenade of Madness

(murmurings from a manic muse)

Angelique M. Gentry

For those who have believed in
and encouraged me in my creative nature
throughout my life. You know who you are,
and you are not forgotten.

Thank you!

Angelique M. Gentry

Special Author's Notes:

Hello! Thank you for purchasing my words. I have written thousands of poems over the years. As I've grown older, and especially in this last year, I find myself teetering between embarrassment and joy when I read my earlier poetry and lyrics. I tell people that poetry need not be perfect to be beautiful. Alas, that is easier for me to apply to other people than myself, and my poetry is very imperfect. However, it does all represent times in my life and in the life of my poetic skill.

I write for the joy of writing. I am very scattered in my style and subject matter. While I've subdivided my poetry into main groupings of subject, attempting to divide it further is more frustrating than useful. It also doesn't represent me. For that reason, this book is likely to be a bit chaotic in its creative expression. That, however, is a good representation of this poet. As those who have followed my writing styles over the years will tell you, my subject matter and style varies from day to day, though I like to think I do have a distinct voice. This book contains poems selected from what I refer to as the "muse" and "magic/fantasy" categories. It does not, however, include my vampire poetry. That will be in a future book. *winkwink*

Any poem or prose that is a "block of text" is intentionally so. Most, I could break down into paragraphs or stanza, but I did not write them that way. I prefer to be authentic to how I write. In this, I ask that you humor me in my debasing of grammar. It's something I do more and more with age, and I've become okay with that.

Angelique M. Gentry

In my personal possession, I have poetry going back some 36 years. There will be a scattering of that throughout these pages. I thought it best, in today's time, to give that varied example. We are constantly growing and changing, yet staying the same. My words will likely showcase that well .

You will find the odd page for your use scattered throughout my book. Creativity has kept me sane and I think it a great medicine in our lives. I am constantly inspired and I enjoy inspiring others with creative prompts. This sharing of creativity is a big part of who I am. For that reason, it is a part of this book. I'll explain a bit more about that on later pages.

I would also like to express my gratitude to the various persons over the years that I've written with or that have given out writing prompts to which I have written to. Some of this poetry likely would not exist were it not for that inspiration. Currently, that includes the many groups on Instagram. Instagram gets a bad reputation for poetry, but there are some truly phenomenal poets on there all inspiring each other. One just has to look for them. Thank you for catching the attention of my muse.

Please enjoy, and if you find yourself inspired... stop reading and scribble away. My poetry isn't going anywhere, but when your muse calls, you should definitely answer.

Angelique

Angelique M. Gentry

Table of Contents

Table of Contents

Angelique M. Gentry

Table of Contents

Table of Contents

Angelique M. Gentry

Table of Contents

Table of Contents

Table of Contents

Table of Contents

Angelique M. Gentry

Moonbeams
spun with spirit's *breath*.
A *tale*
kissed with

the *trust* of a muse.

These lingerings of *imagination*
coax my heart
to *dance*
and *dare* my fingers
to *refuse*.

Angelique M. Gentry

What is poetry? What is madness? What is music? What is art?
What is life? What are dreams?

For this creative spirit, they are more often than not one and the
same.

Every breath. Every heartbeat. Every whisper. Every blink. Every
thought. All of it is poetry. All of it creates a symphony of
possibility within the creative mind. And all of it is universal.

For this reason, I will be including some additional pages
throughout this book so that you can add your own poetry, prose,
and thoughts within its binding. Whether you've written
thousands of poems or have yet to write your first, I hope that
you will make use of the pages. If you do, I would love to see it.
Post a photograph of it on your Instagram account and DM it to
@fromthebreathofdaydreams and I will share it on my stories.

I was warned that I should not do this. That it would possibly
cheapen my book. I think that is utter hogwash. Sharing the love
and encouragement of creativity is one of the most valuable things
in life to me. To have someone moved enough that they would
want to handwrite poetry within the pages of this book would be a
priceless gift, in my mind. That would make me very happy.

So, please, scribble away. Think of this not just as a book of my
poetry, but as a book of our poetry. No two books will be the
same. Kind of like none of us are the same as each other.

May your muse shine brightly! ♥

Angelique M. Gentry

Muse-Touched
Whispers of Madness

(name and date)

Within these pages
lay the murmurings of the muse-blessed.
No two muse are alike,
nor are their blessed.

Please, inscribe your name
and let it be known
that you welcome the creative inspiration
that the Universe deems you to possess.

Angelique M. Gentry

@FromtheBreathofDaydreams

She is always there.
>> Her voice rarely stops.
>>> The *flow* of verse that drifts
>> through my mind could be considered
>>> **madness** by many.
>> To me,
>>> it is *simply life.*
> I am less comfortable
>> when my muse is **silent**
>>> than I am when she's
>>>> rambling non-stop.

My muse *teases and torments* my thoughts
> with possibility.
>> Everything is a daydream
>>> waiting to be **manifested** into reality.
>> Each *smile* is the epitome of giddiness.
Every heartache
> is a gut wrenching debacle of **survival**.
>>> Be it in writing, music, art, or any other
>> form of creativity, my muse is a constant
>>> resource of **curiosity**
>>>> and *wonder.*

I am **lucky**
> to have been driven *insane* by her.
>> Sanity is for the dull-minded
>>> and uninspired.
>> Give me *madness.*
>> Give me *emotions.*
> **Give me** *inspiration*.
>>> Give me *creativity.*
>> It all **balances** out when
>>> we begin...
>>>>> *...again.*

Angelique M. Gentry

Who Am I?

I am...
 ...a moonbeam stolen.
 ...a sloppy semicolon.
 ...a slanted figure eight.
 ...a force you can't negate.

I am...
 ...a humming contemplation.
 ...a slightly strange flirtation.
 ...a soul of silver thread.
 ...a bit of a hothead.

I am...
 ...a rainbow dressed in black.
 ...a vixen on my back.
 ...a bit batty in the attic.
 ...an introverted enigmatic.

I am...
 ...a vulgar scale that wobbles.
 ...a graceful klutz who hobbles.
 ...a tinkering creative.
 ...a bit imaginative.

I am...
 ...a broken wind chime- mended.
 ...a voice not often comprehended.
 ...a melancholy giggle.
 ...a brat who likes to wiggle.

I am...
    ...a playful heart- eclectic.
    ...a puzzle drawn quite skeptic.
    ...a loner too loquacious.
    ...a temple styled curvaceous.

I am...
    ...me.
     a simple oxymoron
     on an unexpected path
     determined to love wholeheartedly.

Angelique M. Gentry

A Poet's Heart

I think within each poet's heart
emotions swirl in rainbow hues.
A need inside sets them apart.
The drive to hear their cherished muse.

And though, with words, they do impart
vast feelings scribed in ink as clues.
It's rare they'll show the voice they chart.
Dictating life to pay their dues.

Metamorphosis

Magic drips and magic flies.
Enchantment lures the old and wise.
Daydreams seed where nightmares bloom.
Beware the sound from a muse's loom.

Moist Remembrance

Entropic cloud dance.
Moist serenade in limbo.
Sorrow drenched Earth song.
Poetry falls in downpours.
Remnants of yesterday's breath.

Recipe for a Poet

A little silly
mixed with sass.
A touch of depravity
tarnished by class.
An ounce of kindness
embellished insane.
Merging opposite poles
is my writing bane.

Sometimes too serious,
frustrated by strife.
Wonder warring with hope.
Dreams that cut like a knife.
Darkness always transcending.
An enveloping home.
Within the paradox of life
is where this poet roams.

Angelique M. Gentry

Song of the Muse

Listen when the madness streams.
Listen when the whispers scream.
Listen to the voices gleam.
Listen to the walking dream.

Be still. Be silent. But don't be meek.
Be aware of what you seek.
Be brave in action. Be unique.
Be confident in your mystique.

Deliver love in all your ways.
Deliver hope. Ignore the craze.
Deliver strength. Set the world ablaze.
Deliver kindness with your praise.

Feel empowered. Take control.
Feel Earth's magic make you whole.
Feel my love. Release the toll.
Feel and reignite your soul.

Haunted

Words
are like the shady whispers
of misbegotten dreams
tiptoeing across the shadows
of my mind.

Every syllable
a hypnotic caress
teasing me with the foreign accent
of stubborn ghosts
who refuse to slumber.

Angelique M. Gentry

Fumbling with Sound and Pen (a song)

Sometimes daydreams weep between the sheets
   of lifetimes never drawn.
Even nightmares sleep on curtains draped
   from memories never sewn.
As the soul departs and spirit rests
   the switchboards can't be stayed.
In this heart, once home of eclipsed pests,
   there's battles to be waged.

Tumbling, tumbling, tumbling 'round again.
Fumbling, fumbling, fumbling with sound and pen.

Mindscapes can evaporate in conditions
   void of charm.
Noon dates barely escape all the pageantry
   of harm.
In the great divide that's caught inside
   others' specters keeping score.
Hardly modesty, claims the token's fee,
   as it's quick to lock the door.

Tumbling, tumbling, tumbling 'round again.
Fumbling, fumbling, fumbling with sound and pen.

Born in madness. Weaned on sadness.
There's a leper at your door.
Can you offer more than empty blessings
   before his hourglass hits the floor?
In the splinters of those captured shards
   lay the seeds to what was lost.
But it's rare to find a willing host
   whose heart will pay the cost.

So, we keep tumbling, tumbling, tumbling 'round again.
Fumbling, fumbling, fumbling with sound and pen.

Rake the grass in phantom whisperings
   still gathered in the moor.
In a boat of careless journeys weave a cascade
   to implore.
Walk the steps tripped in a courtroom
   signed for making peace.
Skip the line that's drawn of fading stones
   'til matters fumble free.

Just keep on tumbling, tumbling, tumbling 'round again.
Fumbling, fumbling, fumbling with sound and pen.

Tumbling, tumbling, tumbling, you tumble, my friend.
We're fumbling, fumbling, fumbling to the end
   ...with sound and pen...to the end...
   with sound and pen...it's the end.

Angelique M. Gentry

Of Salty Ink Splatters

My tired quill has laid to rest
lost sleep from fights of yore.
Bludgeoned tipped to sway my vest
it stains once sound rapport.

Though faulty in its scratch stiff plays
one barters to concede.
The scribbling thoughts have leapt to raze
vast memories once serene.

Weep Not, Vast Dreams Bloom

Weep not these failures staged as gloom.
Without, your ship might sink.
Their presence coax vast dreams to bloom.

Such endings rarely end in doom.
Though cheeks may glow a touch too pink.
Weep not these failures staged as gloom.

Invigorate lost minds to plume.
Set rummage for that missing link.
Their presence coax vast dreams to bloom.

Think broad of what and not of whom.
Until your steps once more do synch.
Weep not these failures staged as gloom.

Refrain from feeding thoughts that fume.
The mind is not a boxing rink.
Their presence coax vast dreams to bloom.

The world is vast and not your tomb.
Though life will take you to the brink.
Weep not these failures staged as gloom.
Their presence coax vast dreams to bloom.

Angelique M. Gentry

#LineBlurrer

Line blurrer.
Spoof disburser.
Bubble popping,
Rhyming curser.
Edge ascender.
Pledged defender.
Challenge taker
on a bender.
High on chuckles.
Could give a fuckles.
That's not true.
Knee often buckles.
Wished a wish upon a star,
then took a dive
to plummet far.
Crowd avoider.
Silent loiter.
Strange, collecting,
art stash sorter.
You say, "hoarder."
I say, "border."
Swaying the scale
of Disorder's order.
Lustful nothing
craving something.
Emancipated.
Could be bluffing.
Loyal to a fault,
but thriving.
Full of shit.
It's called, "surviving."

Has no patience for contriving.
Knows the game,
but won't be driving.
More oft' than not
revivifying.
Leaving
just to keep on striving.
Balanced awkwardly.
Unstable.
Naaa!
That'd mean I wear a label.
Lay the cards out on the table,
there's several lines that I won't cross,
come what may
whate'er the cost.
I won't take a win
if it means being lost...

...but I will keep *blurring* lines.

Angelique M. Gentry

Unraveling Delight

Flaunting sleek.
Stretch supine.
Wonder, sweet wonder.
Enriched and divine.

Awakened from slumber.
Nourished and stoked.
Let the heavens surrender.
Claim the magic invoked.

Fruits of the Feminine

Weep not of your woes,
my goddess child.
'Twas my tears of joy
that rained you
onto Gaea
to heal her pains.

Finish the circle
and blossom
with all the wonder
of the Universe.

Thoughts of a Muse's Concubine

Be gone,
these warring nations reaping havoc upon my soul!
An imbalance of the practical and the divine.
The obsessive realist and the cluttered manic,
both rummaging through the back alleys of thought.
One tidying away, a place for all.
The other stripping to bare bones and sin,
delighted in the orgy of an oncoming creative storm.
It's exhausting, the constant debate of punctual decadence.
Fetching parlour tricks for the uninitiated,
and dallying in the sewage of a leftover trance.
It's neither peaceful nor tranquil.
Just a constant reaping of unreachable transcendence.
Taunting! Taunting! Taunting!
Color blocked and sound deprived.
Brailed whispers screeching at my nerves;
every second an eternity of infinite possibility.
Idea after idea after idea after...
It never stops!
On those rare, blessed moments
where all goes quiet for a few heartbeats
and I can finally breathe;
I'm uncomfortable in the solace of my own skin.
I consider the wisdom of retiring my muse,
and cutting into the conga line of corpses
unhampered by a genius.
But, I know that much like the borg-
resistance is futile.
Besides, I am no more than a balloon
set adrift on the gales of life.
It's her "voice" that gives me direction,
and provides my unraveling path.

Angelique M. Gentry

Still, I wonder what it's like not to be forever tossed about,
catching wave after wave of creation
until blessedly drowning beneath the chaos.
I wonder if it's possible to simply be.

Murmurings of a Waking Muse

Before.
Before the fields swayed blue.
Before the skies danced orange.
Before gold encased the warmth
that cooled our evening songs,
and fever replaced our centers
with a gnawing vacancy.
Before time shattered;
we had learned peace.
Children never wept with hunger,
for our tables were never divided.
Ancient bones only rattled with laughter
in joy with the follies of youth.
They were never disregarded
as little more than wrinkled skin suits
taking up space.
There was knowledge in those fading temples.
Lifetimes of insight to be harvested
and sorted at leisure.
We were bountiful!
We were glorious!
We lived entwined with the rainbow,
instead of chasing it.
We knew our place upon the wheel,
and were respected for how smoothly
we aided in its turning.
We did not just hear the notes of life-
our hearts beat in tune with them.
We were the children of the skies,
and the heavens adored our melodies
for the harmony we sought
with every breath.

Angelique M. Gentry

We were unprepared
for the coming catastrophe.
So content in our journey,
it never occurred to us
that anyone would find our rhythm...
faulty.
We thought...foolishly.
Naively.
Ignorantly.
We thought they would be proud;
Our ancestors.
That we would be valued.
Treasured.
Loved.

Our mistake was in thinking we'd be seen.
We were not.
We were decimated.

Creativity.
Laughter ignited with heart.
Fireworks exploding

Interpreting the Arrangement of an Aging Siren

across these beats my rhythm thrums/ life accelerating in slow
motion/ a melody of hope/ agony relinquished in faltered
abandon/ longing distilled with compassionate determination/ a
foreshadowed, unbecoming, daring me to acquiesce/ to break
mold/ to sunder all scope of retreat/ but I dream/ I dream a
walking dream/ I dream an awakening of perfection/ I dream the
stunted syllable placating its own short-sightedness/ no longer do I
accept the meandering thrum/ no power is spared for the
sharpness of a flat note/ instead, I breathe in/ inhaling the music
of life in all its highs and lows/ and from within myself a voice
emerges/ a confident lyricist/ a melodious chime interweaving all
that is me into an elegantly simple and gregariously complex
musical ensemble/

undertaken by a composer for whom I feel
an absolute absence of separation

Angelique M. Gentry

Morri

Monitoring the evolution of a paper cathedral-
I feel my ink might flow untethered.

Too much knowledge fielding about without a
    reason for sleep.
The concept of responsibility seems an unattainable
    reach.

As clear sighted as a collapsed steeple,
 I fear for the arrest of my imagination.

Colors flutter by.
Kissing flesh with dreams and hope.
So wondrous is art!

Imperfect Heart

There **is** *beauty*

in the *imperfection*

of **the** CREATIVE *heart.*

Don't be afraid
to celebrate
those flaws!

Why not celebrate some now by
scribbling your own poetry and
thoughts on the lines of the next few
pages.

That's right!

WRITE IN MY BOOK!!!

Make it OUR book!

Open up your mind and let your muse
flow free.

Put on some music and just let the
words spill out.

Let them tumble.
Let them flip.
Let them sing.
Ring.
Twirl you into a frenzy of rhyme.

Angelique M. Gentry

<u>Who are YOU?</u>

Self-Pandering

Hyper-vigilant in this reclusive outpouring;
my mind's like a meandering mall rat.
It skitters and splatters across shiny surfaces.
Scratches and squeaks in protest of all restraint.
Restraints, on the other hand, are something
 akin to a bangled jubilee.
A cheeseboard of Hot Topics and Altered Perceptions-
Effortlessly chasing after my kicks into
 inter-dimensional forgetfulness.
Anyone who says, "Diamonds are a girl's best friend."
had to be hanging out at Sears, Roebuck, & Co
 during a "no-money-down" extravaganza.
Just another power tool trying to get a handle
 on the short-circuited.
Resistance is futile! I got a bad desire...
Damn't, Jim. I don't even like Springsteen!
I'm all shook up!
Clearly, the needle on my record is long broken.
Did I mention an affinity for the absurd?
Word choice, that is.
One day, I'll give good diction.

Angelique M. Gentry

Creativity

Turning in circles.
Eager and indecisive.
Boredom's swift descent.

Attention captured.
Something colorful beckons.
Recklessly enthralled.

Insomnia looms.
Chaos sequestered beauty.
Genius consumes all.

Turning in circles.

Anaxiphilia

My heart yearns to quicken, quicken again.
Beyond the pale purgatory of this rapturous cage.
The notes. They thrum in silent reverie.
Cascading then beckoning and lulling to sleep-
the madness.

The sadness.

Encased in gladness that knows no words.
No bounds. They're lost, you see.
It's the cost. The fee.
Forever found inside the leathery fortress
   of my once nimble mind.

It's the sound.

A rhapsody of roaring waves.
A cacophony of Voice titillating my senses
   to surrender to their charm.
Awareness of "reality" a dissonance
   from all I know. All I crave.
All I am brave enough to reach out and touch-
   it's too much.
It's...such...sweet...sweet...sorrow...

Angelique M. Gentry

How it coos and it weeps.
It creeps. It leaps from high to low.
So slow. Never sleeping.
It lunges to stake my escape.
To fake my Inkscape.
My dreamscape. My- *shape.*

ShapeShapeShapeShapeShape

Thoughts agape. Emotions drape.
My soul's awake to the *scrape, scrape, scrape*
   scraping-
Down my spine.
The fine. I must align. I can't unwind.
I must refine. I can't begin to filter harm,
or sound alarm

to the harmony.
The melody.
The whisper never quelled in me.
I am the wailing majesty.
The twice-born, thrice blessed tragedy.
A sharp-shifting landscape carved by a muse
too manic to take a breath.
Overfilled with depth.
Too wide of breadth.

She'll be my death.

She craves the bastion of originality.
And I am but a cracked quartz- forever surfing
the pleasures of misplaced and misbegotten
    treasure
within an ocean of fears too vast
  for one measly scribe to devour.

Uninvited

Rending flesh of fetid breath,
mock tensions tear Fear's tryst.
Cocooned beyond electric mesh,
two dancers' dual persists.

Each round, in substance, air plumes thick,
while lucid fingers sign.
Begone intruding afterthought!
This dreamer's marked divine.

Angelique M. Gentry

The Muse

I am the breath of darkness blooming.
I am the void of night.
I am the kiss of a phoenix crying.
I am the spark that guides your life.

The Inspired

She stood still
chasing circles
in her head.
Avoiding
all the nonsense
spewed
by the voiceless
walking dead.

Brave

Brave the Summer solitude.
Brave your inner child.
Brave the nonsense spewed at you
because others fear what's wild.

The Power of Words

Galaxies envisioned by mere ink on page.
The wispy black line of a life invented,
   or perhaps long-lived.
Only the ancient witness the journey's end;
where words become more than idle suggestion
   or passing thought.
Where a careless conversation
   becomes carved in stone as custom and law,
or the hope of a people becomes mysterious legend-
surrounded in smoke and mirrors, and passed on
   as myth and folklore.
Magic flirts with each syllable spoken,
and illusion dances between scribbled alphabets.
Sounds, familiar and foreign, roll off the toungue
   in mesmerizing cadences
that seep into our subconscious and tattoo our souls
   with ideals and beliefs.

Sometimes dividing. Often uniting.
The power of words knows no equal.

Angelique M. Gentry

These Roads

Around the bend. That time again.
These roads. These roads we travel.
Transitions wrong. To days too long.
These roads. These roads we travel.
Merry be and merry way.
Forgotten blisters gone astray.
Tis Fortune's guard. This boulevard.
Forgotten pains. Still, we restrain.
Let's carry on. Let's sing the song.
Of these roads. These roads we travel.
Go play the part. Resume. Restart.
On these roads.   These roads we travel.

Dream

with all your heart.
For with every beat
it's composing
a *symphony of life*
just for you.

Upon Waking

Such strangled syllables;
mouths agape on hollow truths.
Hallowed ruses running circles
around the chains of life.
Dig deeper! Cut faster!
Slice and dice away all perceptions of reality.
Feeding the fledgling monikers
their uppity ups and tearful tumbles.
Oh, woe is me- this poet's life.
Nurtured on silk sheets and fat-bellied.
The hardships! The heartache!
The struggle of choice!
But I have a dream! ...Damn't, Janet!
Can't we all just plant a seed?
Dare we pause without proceeds?
Fund me! Praise me!
Worship at the altar of my bullshit
and spit shine a glow on this knob
of regurgitated rhetoric.
Been there! Done that! Climbed higher! Fell faster!
Check out these pages,
whipping tears from your eyes;
so swift the demise.
Got that green Cadillac on loan from a shark
with the sharpest smile.
She saw me coming before I tipped that pile.

Angelique M. Gentry

Defiled! Deformed! Dysfunctionally defined!
Got my posse on speed dial,
hooking me up with some of those franchised
hearts-a-glo.
Thumbs up on my shitty flow!
Come on, baby. You know you want a piece
of the action.
A determined hoodwink will always trump
a talented distraction.
So, show me what you're made of, Precious.
I want to see that name shine from Cairo to Cali.
Along the way, go on and toss your soul
in a back alley of forgotten promises
and innocent mistakes.
There's no room for morals
on this fast ride to the fantastic.
Just a slip and a slide, dip and a dive,
fuck the thrive
attitude of self-paced masturbation.
And my hand's just the right size to have you
seeing stars!
Jiggle! Jiggle! Jiggle! Wiggle!
All is not forgotten or forgiven; the forbidden.
Blotched ink-stains scratching at the dovetailed
and derailed scriptures pawned
by the disturbed soul.

Give me those shady characters.
Feed me with vowels that have fallen hard
and fell silent in humbled awe of their surroundings.
Define the abandoned structures left rotting away
from perfectly placed punctuation,
and trap my heart with your scribbled sincerity.
Or just copy and paste, replacing words with haste.
Let your quality be defined by the like-hearted.
There's no room for literary observation
on this shenanigan-filled quagmire of profit.
In conclusion, I'm reminded of a simple song...
Replacing a word helps it to belong.
Can someone please tell me,
"Where have all the real poets gone?"

Inspired?

To be inspired, or to plagiarize?
Why must that be the question?

Angelique M. Gentry

Misidentified Talent

Stop searching
for a new voice
to develop as your own.

Get dirty, gritty,
soft, or witty.
Make a broth,
but of your bone.

It's not unique
to gather up dishes
made with heart
by another's hand.

Instead, with practice
and passionate flare,
find the notes
to your very own band.

My Focus

My focus is like a scattered wind;
dancing through the husks of fallen leaves.
Deliberate. Chaotically despondent.
Resplendissante in its flickering joy.
No surface is safe from its intense scrutiny.
No crack hidden. No flaw unadored.
No perfection left unpulverised.
S, not z, because my focus is an amateur explorer.
Got to get to the guts of the matter.
The sticky bits. The jagged fringe.
The structures glued to keep theft hinged.
Archeological exploration of a mind unwound.
Of an art unfound.
Beyond the buoyancy of a salvaged conflagration,
my focus convulses in a ditch of its own digging.
Choking on the infestation of worms
trying to direct its conduct.
There's no pilots on that twister
of inflated disillusionment.
Only passengers clinging for their lives;
unable to decipher the scrawling aftermath
of a sketch left erased by the pacing of Time.
My focus is a fossilized remnant of a renaissance
kept reclusive.

Angelique M. Gentry

It squats in exhausted splendor
until it huff-n-puffs enough energy
for its next flounce.
My focus is the crosshatched leftovers
from the meanderings of a miscreant muse.
I'm just along for the ride.

Unseen

You like to claim you know me.
Every inch, you say, by heart.
But you've barely scratched the surface,
for you do not see my art.
How can you think to recognize?
For I just can't understand
your lack of care about the words I write,
or what's created by these hands.

Keeping Score

Rebellious font.
Side-stepping paused cues.
Backspacing across engorged emotions.
Parallel parking beside memories best kept
frozen beyond Time.
How luxuriously your ink flows.
Do spare a blotted line to source
an evaporated retirement.

Illusionary Vibes

The amplified obstruction
left us teetering with anticipation.
Come closer. Drift lighter.
Sing your song. Be free.
Creative reproduction
underlying all that jazz.
Quiet tamber. Feel the bass calm.
Engineer some harmony.

Angelique M. Gentry

What's in a Name?

A constant poke
to instigate action.
Page possibilities;
nonrestrictive,
but heartfelt.
Luring thought,
though clearly too long.
The unfinished journals.
The unforgettable songs.

These Pages

These pages,
scribbled and torn,
bled through
and illegible
-weathered, frayed,
and stained with life-
tell the greatest story
I will ever know.

Scraps

scraps of torn colors
creativity bleeding
life tenders fuel from within

Fibers

colorful fibers
acceptance bound in frayed knots
dreams manifested

Worlds

Worlds woven with love.
Poetry painted with care.
Witness my heart's dance.

Wishes Granted

Transformed overnight.
Awoke with wishes granted.
Colors paint my life.

Angelique M. Gentry

Accepting Me

I lay in bed with itchy dread
and joy bubbling abundant.
Uncomfortable, but hard of head.
I refuse to be made redundant.
I think of life and the lessons learned
as well as the ones still brewing.
It's strange to understand what's churned
on this path I'm still pursuing.
I'm nothing like I once aspired.
My views on life- long shifted.
The jargon termed "success" retired.
My goal post has since drifted.
I am but a simple soul
with dreams of happy endings.
These broken pieces now made whole
have merged into thoughtful blendings.

Nebulous Static

Damp transgressions entice
chilled heart. Rolling.
Roaring. Ricocheting rowdy ruminations
to part with their mystery.
Surging the threads of joy with misery.
Countless histories chime to blend
bygone sound with
a plethora of future's choice-
Sowing seeds of fictional voice.
Vacillating rhythms with rubix flare.
Care. Dare. Beware. Despair.
Deliberately drown in decadent noise
until silence weighs mute screams.
Rejoice!

Contemplating a Spent Pen

Why sifts between the midnight brews
where bitter drops fall sweetly.
Overtly flaunting when swept rues
with letters smudged discreetly.

Each subtle curve so neatly squared
mends borrowed moments guarded.
Frame open arms when ink's repaired
staves flee departure's parted.

Angelique M. Gentry

Tuned In

Contemplating anxiety.
A compilation I can pen.
To round the page
or disengage?
Why can't ink comprehend?
A loosened screw?
Some half-baked tell?
Must noise siege every crack?
Step-by-step, eyes front.
Mind fed.
I'd rather sidle back.
Wall up and shield.
Assure mask firmly placed.
Dissipate the chaos
seeping into bubbled space.
Pause as tempo faulters.
Resist the urge to shift a note.
Resistance can be futile,
but getting stuck can alter scope.
Perfection's non-existent.
So much feeds to scatter form.
Love ensures the soul stays buoyant.
Life impedes to scratch heart worn.
Numb it down.

Then numb some more.
Engage mind blinds.
Ground through the floor.
Open shutters to siren's blare.
Negate the screams.
Exhale. Repair.
Contemplating anxiety;
A compilation I can pen.
While others always come and go.
It remains my closest friend.

Particled refuge.
A cascade of domed madness.
Sequels temporized.
Life escapes the Sands of Time.
Daydreams can't be bound by law.

Angelique M. Gentry

Constructive Ruin

Tear it down to build it up.
Break the mold and ruck the muck.
Rip the seams then bind with dare.
Slice each cut to release and flare.

Destruction is your love language.
It's spoken from the heart.
For every garnered piece you draft
creates a brand-new start.

There's beauty in the shambles.
Obliteration of the sum.
A collaborative amble
between yourself, what's broke, and fun.

Interrupted Dessication

Elongated wisdom.
Thick rooted in sepulture's prism.
Life dangles in the unbecoming.
The unthreading.
The cataclysmic evolution of more.
Splintered crumbling remakes voice.
Restakes choice in the rendered altruism
crawling, creeping, tunneling away.
Interceding in death's delivery.
Interfacing with life's epiphanies.
Intermingling in interstellar ideation.
Genius succumbs.
Always succumbs.
For inspiration is a quivering hold
enthusiastically emboldened
by delight.

Sleep
-sometimes-
embraces a very good night.

Angelique M. Gentry

Into the Dreaming

Tide walks.
Sashaying across parched plains in solemn
steps.
A rebirth- Uninhibited.

Searching. Sweeping.
Gathering seeds, the gardener watches.
Masquerading as ordinary- There is no such
thing.

A simple question of youth.
The answer a truth seemingly unliked.
All becomes revealed- Over time.

Gaiety unfolds.
Across ancient limbs. Upon ivory steps.
Friendship bonds studies- divergence glows.

Digressing Signals

In times at night, I gale dissent,
The spawned half-life unfounded.
Through wasting waters, adrift to steal,
Disturbed, I surge surrounded.

Not sand, nor hilltop, moped in tar
Might pluck my filtered borrow.
Sputtered reckless in rhapsodic flint
I navigate shod morrow.

Profusion shackles sap in tints,
Though color scapes obsessions.
Sleep loiters on the flaming slate.
Bids dieu, these smoke seamed lessons.

Good Vibrations

Excitement escalates.
Randomized rhyming rolls wistful.
Some mornings just start off
with smiles on high beam.
What an enjoyable trill.

Butterflies frolicking
deep within the pit of stagnation,
evoke excited dance.

Angelique M. Gentry

Colorfully Me with a Periwinkle Splash

Abstruse evocations oscillate my mind sublime.
Re-imagined and intangible-
In the colors, eye-defined.
Pigmented possibilities portraying Patchwork
To Penelope Popsocks.
Teach flow and let go in quilted soul
Palpitating my neural rocks off.

ahem

Zaffre's a bit zany in his vibrant need to flare.
Celeste is more subdued in her subtle sweep of care.
Delft is understated, always striving for the calm.
Smalt's combobulated, adding depth to temper balm.

Falu flaunts with barnyard quips.
While Caput Mortum teases Death.
Bole is blah, but added fun.
Oxblood might be my number one.

(Ssshhh! Don't tell Alizarin Crimson! She might fade away!)

Of all these personalities, from Bubblegum to Bleak,
There's one group that you might have guessed
Who make my life complete.

Phlox is a quick wake me up.
Her demeanor oh so bright.
Murasaki melts across my wall,
Providing magic to my night.
Puce provides the perfect blush
When shade rejects the pretties.
Jacaranda interjects a blue
To balance out life's confetti.

Periwinkle, it must be stated,
Is my color love.
Sure, I enjoy the dark, obscure,
But she floods my soul with love.
We often dance in gleeful sway
To chimes heard only on the breeze.
Through gardens perfumed disarray
And across lush fields toward painted seas.

Yes, I wallow in the bleak of Noir,
Perverse in light's sweet absence.
But Periwinkle's always there
To 'scape life with distractions.
She fits in with most everything,
Painting thoughts to sparkle fluid.
And tugs me from perfection's clutch
Reminding there's beauty in the lurid.

Angelique M. Gentry

For it's not how it's said or how it's worn.
It's not superficial or skilled distract.
True artistry begins the day we're born.
When there's only emotion and little tact.
The colors of my mind are masked
In layers so deep I drown.
I wonder of the adventurer who'd dare
The maze pigmenting that life of sound.

Until I stumble 'pon such fool
Who sees beyond the scare,
And doesn't get so caught up
In the who, what, when, and where.
I have my pretty Periwinkle,
Demanding I stay free,
And paint and write what flares inside,
For being me is a wonderful place to be.

Be

Be always drunken.
Be always high.
Be always eager to touch the sky.

Be always curious.
Be always stirred.
Be always rapt to smudge a line blurred.

Be all ways and always and small ways adept.
Smell the lure and procure every joy sung and wept.
Be salacious, audacious, and gracious to swoon.
Speak voracious, tenacious, and capacious of loon.

Be...most important...BE present in mind.
Be intoxicated in the now and leave the past far behind.
Be hopeful of the future.
Be avarice to entice every crumb of every experience
of every sorrow and every vice.

Be always spirited.
Be all ways just you.
Be absorbent of the old.
Be enraptured with the new.

Angelique M. Gentry

Be in love with love and love as you can.
Be the laughter in tears.
Be the tears in the sand.
Be the fearless song coaxing joy to greedily share.
Be united in heart.
Be enthusiastic in dare.

Be. Just be.
Let life fill in the rest.
Whether high or low-
Be always drunken and crest.

Contemplating Self

Forever at war-
this yin and yang.
Superseding balance to regain the claim;
To my life.
My joys.
My fears.
My fate.
Why can't they work together
and optimize this crumbling slate?

Upon Waking Wishes

I wish my passion would return
instead of nightmares jarring.
To fall asleep, not jerk awake
from images long marring.
To feel the urge to not withdraw.
To leap with both eyes open.
I wish for things I'll never have
then settle with my coping.
I think, sometimes, that life has passed.
I let my daydreams fizzle.
I logic down a morose path
instead of kindled sizzle.
I smile and disassociate
for what is life but sadness?
I wish my brain would just unlearn
and wallow in its madness.

Reboot

I find this moment periodic.
Unknown elements; new and refined.
A by chance blending turned rhapsodic.
This unlocking of my mind.

Angelique M. Gentry

Illiterate Shelves

The silent howl
is a constant thunder
raging war
against the vacant shelves
in this library gone illiterate.

The Man

Such mad men held in stations loft.
Their sad hearts paint our woes.
Those glad men found in pages oft
share tales to trick our foes.

But one man, wise and slick with glee.
His pen scribed stories- true.
That one man, Stan, whose last name's Lee-
to the world gave all he knew.

I Did Not Find Poetry

I did not find poetry. Poetry found me-
   a skinned-knee romantic of melancholy.
An emotional construct unequipped to express
   the bombardment of moments
   both exhumed and repressed.

I do not write poetry. I dictate a voice-
   a bountiful chorus bloomed
   from constraint and choice.
A weaver whose threads tie a scene with a thought.
   placing mirrors in corners
   meant to beckon what's sought.

I did not choose poetry. I surrendered my mind-
   to a compass thrice-flipped for the souls
   left behind.
There's a kindness interwoven with the bleak
   and the cruel
   coaxing nightmares and daydreams
   to merge on life's spool.

I do not claim poetry. My soul bleeds it in trade-
   a foundational conundrum,
   veiled to merge and cascade.
Beyond the faulty inflation of a lock without key.
   I did not find poetry. Poetry found me.

Angelique M. Gentry

@FromtheBreathofDaydreams

Touched with Genius

Please use the following handful of pages to write your own muse-touched poetry and thoughts. Let your mind speak freely and allow the syllables to flow onto the page. Don't be precious in worrying about making a mistake. Poetry is made of mistakes. That's what makes it so incredible. Let your creativity flourish and feel the wonder of being inspired.

Do you find it challenging to think of something to write about, or do you just enjoy being prompted? After I provide a few pages for you to do your own thing, I'll add some with muse/creativity inspired prompts to get your ink flowing.

Is your muse captivating? Describe him/her/
them in a poem.

Think about how your muse influences you and write a poem describing it.

Think about a poet who has a writing style you admire. Craft a poem in that style.

Play with sound as you write this poem. What would your muse sound like singing it?

Be evocative. Be mysterious. Be provocative. Invoke your inner Poe punk and go wild!

A
Murmuring
of
Magic

Do you **believe** in those
creatures who *sparkle* in the night?
How about the ones who **dapple** the
daylight with darkness?
Do you have **magic** *flowing* in your pen?
Would you like to?
I would! Maybe one day I will.
Maybe one day **WE** will!!!

Angelique M. Gentry

There is magic in the maddened mind. Oh, yes! Glorious, exciting, freeing magic. What more enchanting gift exists than to be able to carry ourselves anywhere throughout all of space and time within the blink of an eye?

Words might just be the most magical thing in all of existence...

Whether charming or frightening, electrifying or underwhelmingly mundane- magic comes in all shapes and sizes.

Please allow me to share with you some of the magic my muse shares with me. The magic in nature, love, vampires, and comedy will be in future books. As will other topics. For now, please enjoy the fantasy that lay between these pages.

Angelique M. Gentry

Beckoning Moonlight

Gloom betrays theft's brighter daze.
The haze kept nondescript.
Worrying, wandering, waning away.
Thy moonlight's tip has dipped.

Crowing bothers crown's remorse.
Soothed, they scratch and bay.
Sticks that stab might sting with force.
When sorrow looms to stay.

Plow into theft's wintered slumber.
Yawn this maw of gain.
Howl beyond felled silver's sunder.
Cleave thy heart's abstained.

Waning Life

Moon blind travesty.
Synopsis burned in silver.
Thistles fade to blight.
Bruised beneath sky's haunted eyes.
Arcane memories crumble.

Angelique M. Gentry

I

Drenched in sorrow.
Lost in time.
I'm a wanderer
of lust and grime.

Through heaven's gates,
I stormed and fell.
I'm the writer of histories
that others tell.

In my footprints there is madness.
I'm the keeper of despair.
While king and country fight in battles,
I'm the god who hears their prayers.

My voice beckons to the tortured.
I'm a lunatic of verse.
Carved of hatred, greed, and malice,
only truth is more perverse.

Guard your loved ones from my wisdom.
Hide your children from my care.
While others speak of honor,
I suckle nightly on despair.

If the world's really but your oyster,
I hold the pearl within my hand.
The hour of reckoning is upon you,
and your fate is my command.

The Storm

Fare thee well, my wicked friends.
A storm is coming which marks the end.
We cannot live.
We cannot die.
Shall we pray
or bow our heads and just sigh?

Triad

with *Sadness* comes *Knowledge*
with *Knowledge* comes *Power*
with *Power* comes more *Sadness*

Angelique M. Gentry

Sunset at Midnight

Sunset at midnight.
Sunset at dawn.
Sunset to life is an unfinished song.
We dance for tomorrow.
We dance for today.
We dance for the sightless-
the hags who hold sway.

Balanced pendulum.
Rhythmic in tomorrow's dream.
Poised Imperfection.
Regret rules fears.
Ancient whispers offer hope.

Nightfall envelops.
Descending dreams escape strife.
Starlit ascension.
Shadows soothe the reigning depths.
Balance lulls chaos to sleep.

Lavender Fields

Sleep, daughter, sleep.
Come and rest your eyes.
For your journey is long,
and your life's filled with spies.
It is only in dreams
where our spirits may meet.
In this bi-fractal world
are the answers you seek.

Sleep, daughter, sleep.
You must remember the way.
Just how many more lifetimes
do you intend to pay?
Into the lavender fields
that you helped us to sow,
is where this journey must end.
It's where I need you to go.

Sleep, daughter, sleep.
There's not else you can do.
The decision's been made.
Now the round's come anew.
Why must you tarry with hope
when you know it's the end?
Have you learned nothing more
from that test you've named friend?

Angelique M. Gentry

These Dreams

These dreams. These dreams caught stranded.
These dreams left to be frail.
These dreams once thought demanding.
These dreams lost on that trail.

When all we were was magic.
When all we felt was tragic.
Gone are blue skies
fled from grey eyes.
Gone is all we once thought true.

You said our dreams. Our dreams were castles,
    just waiting for us to come home.
Our dreams could cross vast oceans,
    just skipping like a stone.
Our dreams were milk and honey, smooth and silky,
    warm and sticky sweet.
Our dreams were chasing four leaf clovers;
    green grass cold beneath our feet.

But gone is all that power that once sparkled in the sun.
Gone. Gone. Gone is our little merry-go-round.
Too much spinning just ain't fun.

Those flies like syrup on your lips.
Despising their rough fingertips.
From mountain highs to valley lows;
all the tap, tap, tapping on each other's toes.
We flashed like lightning and burned to dust.
Ashes to ashes, all we do is fuss.
So goodbye, Johnny. Goodbye, Sam.
   Goodbye, Marge and goodbye, Cam.

Oh, these dreams. These dreams- they sparkle.
These dreams filled with mystique.
These dreams aren't patriarchal.
These dreams will stay unique.

When all I am is magic.
I won't let this life be tragic.
'Cause these dreams are grey skies
loved by blue eyes
waking up to truth.

Angelique M. Gentry

Morose Musical

Moonbeams caught dancing.
Chilled cellists listen.
The rhythm's spun haunting.
Crapehanger eyes glisten.

Fingers fly fretful.
Strings serenade heartache.
Alone with their music.
Sad songs lure to partake.

Infrequent rhythms.
Allusion to convert.
Hedonistic timing.
The death maiden's concert.

The Blinding of Light

Whisper,
once in grief,
cliches.
Entwine this darkened light;
A paradox
most ruse as day.
Fletched arrows
pawned in blight.
One man of many faces-
true.
Dark hunter touched with gold.
While graceful versed,
your heart beats skewed.
Apollo,
the mistold.

Angelique M. Gentry

Grasping Mindfulness

Of captured words that flit through mind
and set lost soul to quest.
Enraptured yearnings drawn to kind
endearments' careful zest.
This wandering wonder, wildly waning
whispers wistful wants.
Determined zest to discard Fate's
entrapments and uncage haunts.

Drawing Life

Through times race, passed.
Once three. Not five.
We faltered breath.
We slept. Alive.
Thine doom. My beacon.
My pace. His brew.
Our slumber's spent.
We're sketched anew.

Upon Waking Effigy

Howling riverbed.
Transactions teetering
in a nightingale's solemn embrace.
These bandages lay restless;
Listless pebbles plunging to their deaths.
Kerplunk! Kerplunk!
Strike a match
and **BURN!**
Kindle the superficial soul into a roaring fire.
Let loose the twigs and bramble.
Hideaway! Fly away!
Spark upon that ebon shore.
Rake floundering flesh with the barbs of experience.
Lay *shallow* and *wilt.*
Ferny fingers stretching outward,
seeking the damp ruins of a forgotten inferno.
Bask upon the effigy
of a life squandered with the tides,
and **rise, spirit rise!**
Go forth and seek enlightenment.
Wade within the *footsteps* of a **Universal Dream.**

Angelique M. Gentry

Lunar Awareness

Vagrant flowers
steeped with intrusion.
Conspired and myopic
the migrating illusion.
Condensation rued in the mysteries
fled from a harbinger's sail-
lost in glee.

Drowned in frowns the
buttercup does melt.
Felted cisterns berating the once thought svelte.
All the throng worshiped wrong
in a song rarely delt
to the few who could hear-
the notes chiming.

Low tides row
churning the sources
of nourished seeking
absence in voices.
Blown by the foolish retorts
to a droned miss-eating mob
of surfs too bored-
to bloom or swoon.

Their doom. There's doom in...

Vagrant flowers
speak disillusion.
Contrived to peek
in the foals once thought lucent.
Masquerade's sapling rooting
a new stint to plug
the anguish-
a crew accrued.

It's time to sing adieu.
Memories rarely brew-
Out of sight.
Out of mind.
Out of time.
Out of rhyme.
Out of luck.
Out of choice.
Out of courage to rejoice.
Out of all of the rotating dreams locked in fervor.
Out of voices too quiet to linger and savor.

The cherished pangs of life.
The cherished pang of life-
to Night...
tonight.

Angelique M. Gentry

A Melody for Darkness

Darkness falls before the sun.
He wraps his arms around everyone.
Darkness is a cold embrace.
Intimate with a touch of grace.
Darkness sings and Darkness calls.
He breaks the rules. He's beyond all laws.
Darkness stalks beyond the gates.
Unfettered by those vindictive fates.
Darkness is my one true friend.
Within his arms all the madness ends.
Darkness takes careful care of me.
Blocking out all light, so that I might see.
Darkness comes and Darkness goes.
He rolls through the streets to collect our woes.
Darkness waits deep inside our minds.
To eat away all the ties that bind.
Darkness trades in tales of mystery.
He's a promise woven from past tragedies.
Darkness wounds and Darkness flays.
His prison's made of yesterdays.
Darkness never breaks his chains.
He bends until he becomes his pains.
Darkness holds the key to all our hearts.
Unlocking fears to give us brand new starts.

Darkness laughs and Darkness cries.
Misunderstood, he's been framed by lies.
Darkness turned the other cheek.
He built up his walls to defend the meek.
Darkness waits and Darkness sleeps.
My eternal light. Darkness plays for keeps.

Fading Silhouette

Haunting stones weep from the deadly malaise
of an ascension of abominations
that ransacked my grace.

It was grueling. So wondrous- the unsanctioned start
needing ink-stained fingers
and a flaming heart.

I bartered with horrible sanity stricken
to turn back the hand of a tock
that keeps tickin'.

Life finds a way to feed the possessed-
'neath the splendid ruins
of a soul once obsessed

Angelique M. Gentry

The Banshee Wailed (a song)

It wasn't like other mornings.
The sky was the wrong shade of blue.
Lines, once crossed, no longer had shape.
There was nothing left she could do.

The water that ran was a beckoning.
Yet she couldn't see what came before.
The crosses she wore from goodbyes never told
were the whispers that echoed her roar.

And the banshee wailed with the morning light.
Drenched in fear, she scrubbed to forget the signs.
Of the pain. So much pain. So much pain that she
    felt.
Void of life. Void of hope. Void of all but the jail.

Of the bitterness. Of the breaks yet to come.
Of the sorrow staining the hymn that she hummed.
Of the ever afters that never would pass.
Of the corpse she became on that field holding mass.

Yeah, the banshee wailed...with the morning light.
All the hearts she would break...took away her fight.
So, the banshee wailed... yeah, the banshee cried.
Hoping one. Maybe one. Just one battered soul
would hear her heartache and choose not to go.

Maybe it wouldn't be...if only they'd see.

Blood was the beacon that called her.
Stuck to the feathers and bones flocked for sport.
Agony whistled through the clouds floating by.
Terrifying the vessels before she'd report.

"Beware the washer woman!"
A warning her victims would moan.
Running away, towards the doom of her song.
Thinking she was the reason they weren't going
    home.

So the banshee wailed with the morning light.
Drenched in fear, she scrubbed, to forget the sight.
Of the pain. So much pain. So much pain that they
    felt.
Void of life. Void of hope. Void of all but the jail.

Angelique M. Gentry

Of the bitterness. Of the breaks yet to come.
Of the sorrow staining the hymn that she hummed.
Of the ever afters that never would pass.
Of the corpse she became on that field holding mass.

Yeah, the banshee wailed...with the morning light.
All the hearts she would break...took away her fight.
And the banshee wailed... yeah, the banshee cried.
Hoping one. Maybe one. Just one battered soul
would hear her heartache and choose not to go.

Maybe, this time, it wouldn't be...if only they'd see...
if only they could see she.

The droplets dripped. Dripped. Dripped into water.
That ran red with blood. Blood. From all the fodder.
Mixed with salt she cried. Cried. To unbind them.
And the flesh she plied. Plied to sanctify them.

It's said that she gave up her soul
on a field lost to memory.
In hopes that some could go
live beyond the violent sentry.
Bargained life for bone;
the rules demanded she must greet them.
Offer up clean clothes
washed sacred in the blood that could release them.

That's why the banshee wailed with the morning light.
Drenched in fear, she scrubbed, to forget the sight.
Of the pain. So much pain. So much pain that she felt.
Void of life. Void of hope. Void of all but the jail.

Of the bitterness. Of the breaks yet to come.
Of the sorrow staining the hymn that she hummed.
Of the ever afters that never would pass.
Of the corpse she became on that field holding mass.

Yeah, the banshee wailed…with the morning light.
All the hearts she would break…took away her fight.
So the banshee wailed…yeah, the banshee cried.
Hoping one. Maybe one. Just one battered soul
would hear her heartache and choose not to go.

Maybe it wouldn't be…If only they'd see.

It wasn't like other mornings.
The sky was the wrong shade of blue.
Lines, once crossed, no longer had shape.
There was nothing left she could do.

Angelique M. Gentry

Loosening Love-Me-Knot

Begone damned soul that haunts mine prime.
Pray still thy voice against mine ear.
This heart beats cool to yonder's fear.
Thy mountain I no longer climb.

Deception's claused to pantomime.
Lay ceased as mine death draws to near.
Begone damned soul!

Their squalling reeks of paradigm.
Long-suffered venom fades to clear.
Beware there is no welcome here.
As soul escapes unwind this crime.
Begone damned soul!

The Unique Horn

My lover ran away last Summer, beneath the
    flailing lullaby of a sacrificial moon.
I cut a hole in the twisted beat of my sleeve
    to pattern a cause for the wound.
Stitch-by-stitch those shards of ice teared up
    to soak my pelt.
But like my lover, sun-kissed thrice, the salt-soaked
    sheets taught my pain to melt.

We weren't the tragic souls half met. You know,
    the ones still blind with need.
We were fragrant in our desires;
    the pollened vessels bound to seed.
Upon a yarrowed path, unkempt with footsteps,
    our tumbling benedictions stilled.
He, with eyes of soil unswept, turned twice my way
    and vowed to yield.

I was captured. Shackled true. Ensnared by lips
    that yet to speak.
Lush with bounty and curved on end;
    they carved the most entrancing peak.
And when they parted, to sing with voice,
    like maple stretching for my tongue.
My lifebeat stumbled to respark
    a brand new journey to begin.

Angelique M. Gentry

My lover's earthbound, with leg count two
    and sparse in hair, I do attest.
But it curls up wild and free, black as night,
    and filled with cheeky jest.
His flesh has been toasted nutmeg warm;
    both in color and in touch.
It rippled prickly when he saw me,
    confessing ardor, I know that much.

I heard his heartbeat skip a song.
    His breath turned quick with lust.
I preened beneath the moon, hung high,
    ensorcelling his trust.
His gestures slowed in reverence,
    such a sight I was to see.
With entrapped gaze, my knees met earth,
    to draw him close to me.

I felt the dewdrops lick my flesh
    with kisses from the breeze.
My ears turned to the timid dance
    that stuttered lofty trees.
My lover didn't seem to care
    which audience we drew.
His eyes had sight for me alone,
    caring not if sky stayed blue.

And so, I froze upon that mound,
  swayed curious enough to speak.
My tongue, untied, caused his to bind,
  and somehow stalled him meek.
Within worn hands that trembled so,
  I watched him grasp hard steel.
By flick of thumb and scrape of cloth,
  inch-by-inch he did reveal.

My lover's sword is bold and long.
  It glistens to the tip.
I've yet to see another blade
  of such fine craftsmanship.
So confident was his approach;
  I think he found me weak.
Instead, I thought to simply rest
  and adore his toned physique.

The birds had stopped their serenade
  as if they knew which steps he'd take.
A pair of cardinals went to seed;
  predicting his mistake.
And so, I met those dirt dark eyes-
  lined ghostly by the moon.
I listened to the charm he spoke.
  It had a catchy tune.

Angelique M. Gentry

When last he chose, upon my breast,
   to vigorously thrust.
I turned my head, with neck kept bare,
   and offered him my trust.
My lover could have stopped his strike.
   His stance was balanced firm.
Instead, he screamed, as was his right,
   and caused my legs to squirm.

Each blow of cord-whipped strength was met.
   He danced a jaunty jig.
Our blood, which flowed on ground still damp,
   soon painted moss-specked twig.
If only he had stilled that hand,
   and gentled his first stroke.
I could have calmed the raging beast
   such callous care had woke.

Once finished with our waltz of lust,
   we stared with souls stripped bare.
My lover's wound, a death blown crutch,
   ran deep with my despair.
The forfeit of air I'd yet to breathe
   seemed an easy sacrifice.
For what's eternity, but hell,
   if deprived your paradise?

My lover chose to slip away
    like moonlight fleeing dawn.
I waited, mane shorn short with grief,
    to see what death might spawn.
Unique, my horn had fit him well,
    but ruined our chance to mate.
For love's a cruel misanthrope
    to those birthed rare by fate.

Angelique M. Gentry

The Catticorn

She spins and ascends through the darkest of plights.
She whirls and unfurls to reach uncharted flights.
She dives deep and sweeps low to face agony's zest.
She's a loon when morose and a vamp at her best.

She's conniving to tickle a grin from The Grimm.
She enlivens the fickle to befriend their chagrin.
She's a glorious scamp just a trotting along.
She's one reason I'm enlightened to entice the Sun's song.

She is wondrously whimsical and wantonly warm.
She woos the rabid to peace and sings the passive to storm.
She's a puzzle who pieces every quandary a fix.
She's got a thing for the shadows and swims in the Styx.

She might be a heathen, but that crazy's got class.
She's a teensy bit sweet with a whole lot of sass.
She stays drunk in her zeal to shake off all scorn.
She's a rambunctiously sought after, drunk catticorn!

Winter is Coming

You must dare not heed the harbingers.
Their words are poison to the sane.
Don't give weight to all their warnings.
Though she comes this way again.

I hear the wolves across the mountains.
Their howling taunts the frightened prey.
Those melodies sing sweet of heartache.
And of the bite they bring this way.

Once warm at heart, it's said she loved him.
Their romance swept Summer from his feet.
It mattered not, those honeyed whispers.
There was a test she must defeat.

With childish torment, the Fates play cruel.
Their amour propre is legend wrote.
These two, in love, so sure to victor.
Failed to heed the warning quote.

In but a moment, hope was slaughtered.
Their futures torn in Hyemal's hand.
Summer turned his back, tumultuous.
While his lady fought to stand.

Angelique M. Gentry

Buried deep in harsh reflection.
Their struggles twined in duty's knot.
The lovers split, with hearts torn sunder.
Our lady paused and sheltered rot.

His court lay fluid in indulgence.
Their excessive joy cannot be bound.
For sunshine gleams when left unhindered.
It lights the skies and paints the ground.

No longer dormant; winds turn chilly.
Their song's crescendo impends new life.
Pray your ruler's grown in wisdom.
And has the strength to touch his wife.

A Sacrificial Threading

Once upon a nightmare-swindled,
beyond the quagmire of a forsakened morning,
I stood perplexed.
Slightly vexed.
Indiscriminately hexed via a thoughtless complex
of intermediary confessions.
The meandering duress,
while solicitated as a test,
had the atmospheric quality
of a church mouse tendering
sly concessions... Lessons
bound within the intricacy of lust's tides.
Hopeful escapisms
mounting tomfoolery across a parched domicide.
Bide. Bide.
Bide to provide
the divide of their snide
and churlish obsessions- lingering,
ever fingering the naughty notes whimpered
on a scale of half-baked transgressions.
Swooning impressions.
Cloistered discretions- amplified
and soundlessly wrung,
or superstitiously spun,
upon the raging snout
of a minotaur's dwindling libido.

What did he know?

A lot!

Rather labyrinthine- their plot
to ensure he rot for refusing to trot
to their cowardly wrought,
pride drenched, and unsought suppression.
Unencumbered by their aggression,
and slightly amazed
by the vast display of obsession
over his birth earned possessions,
the not-so-menacing serenader
of the salaciously serendipity hoof-scooted his way
beyond their breach of trust-
as often one must when confronted
with a lack of progression towards all things venery,
and retreated into a shadowy bliss
they bemoaned as squalor.
Such a torturous tale,
albeit far from stale-
for one can never tell in the search of tail,
whether the pious
will grab a bull by the horns
or condemn him to retreat in dejected forlorn.

Angelique M. Gentry

All I know is...

Once upon a nightmare-swindled,
beyond the quagmire of a forsakened mourning,
I stood perplexed.
Slightly vexed.
And unabashedly, most candidly, unapologetically
transfixed.

A Deadly Memory

His kiss still tastes of nightshade
as it lingers on mine lips.

The tingles of amour
doth spread and tickle at the tips.

Confession comes quite easy
once soft earth has greeted spade.

Behold the violet splendor
of the final bed he's laid.

Past Imperfect Spoilers-
Just Beyond the Veil of Reality

Past imperfect... our life stuttered.
Past imperfect... all time shuttered.
Past imperfect... Silence taunted.
Past imperfect... spoilers haunted.
Past imperfect... when I met you.
Past imperfect... what we'd go through.
Past imperfect... books came calling.
Past imperfect... was our falling.
Past imperfect... Doctor, listen.
Past imperfect... your decision.
Past imperfect... mad man boxed tight.
Past imperfect... was our last night.
Past imperfect... when you caught me.
Past imperfect... oh, what we'd see.
Past imperfect... life must keep score.
Past imperfect... cracks you deplore.
Past imperfect... our life stuttered.
Past imperfect... all time shuttered.
Past imperfect... Silence taunted.
Past imperfect... spoilers haunted.

Hello, Sweetie!

Angelique M. Gentry

The Dance

Beyond the violent sigh of chance.
Where stardust blinds what pains.
The Universe led us to dance.

It seemed a slight of happenstance.
A mockery to open vein.
Beyond the violent sigh of chance.

Our love was Luna's death romance.
Mad rhythms bound insane.
The Universe led us to dance.

Each twirl entwined our hearts' expanse.
This voyage of Love's domain.
Beyond the violent sigh of chance.

Time fluttered past our entwined stance.
For us there was no strain.
The Universe led us to dance.

Yet Space and Time ne'er do explain.
Some orbits go askance.
Beyond the violent sigh of chance.
The Universe taught us to dance.

Don't Blink

I met him once...
In what seems like another lifetime. Another face.
Another place. Another moment- lost.

The Doctor.

Being his companion comes at a cost, you see.
He'll act like it's forever. He'll make you feel
like you're the center of the Universe.
He'll spend every moment of all of time with you,
and claim it's still not enough.
That he needs more. More. So much more.

Oh, the adventures! The excitement! The
dreams just waiting to be explored.
We had... fun;
The Doctor and I.
We just clicked, you know?
Great minds and all of time.
What could possibly go wrong?

Time. Timing. Mortality. The Master.
He doesn't like endings
and he's very good at running-
from one place to the next.
One face to the next.

Angelique M. Gentry

Each equally important.
Each the best moment ever.
Isn't he clever?

The Doctor.

One day, you'll gaze into his eyes and see
the entire Universe ablaze.
He'll smile that mad smile and you'll feel your
very breath pause in wonder.
He'll grin. He'll wink. He'll exclaim how utterly,
brilliantly perfect you are.
He'll kiss you and share... everything.
And nothing.
Because as soon as you agree to step into his space.
His place. His box.
Oh, that box!

Out of the blue, he'll be gone.
Just like that.
Seconds will tick and you'll wait.
Minutes come and hours go. You'll wait.
Days turn to nights and nights to weeks. You'll
worry, but wait.
Weeks to months. Months to years. Years to...
Did it ever even happen?

That time. Those moments.
The stolen heartbeats lost within a universe of silence.
Was he even real?

The Doctor.

He makes sure you'll never forget him,
because he won't remember you beyond one
blink and the next.
It's not the Weeping Angels that you should
fear when you close your eyes.
It's the clever, clever boy who's always
running...
... always... running...
...always exchanging faces...
...always seeking the next great adventure...

Don't think for one moment that loving him
makes you special.
That him loving you makes you special.
It doesn't.
Loving the Doctor is like loving a star.
He shines for everyone, and everyone seeks out
that light in the darkness
because when he glows- oh, how he glows.

Angelique M. Gentry

But when he goes dark…
…you'll never see him again.
Not if he can help it.

Hello, Sweetie.
Remember me?
I'm still waiting.

Season of

Crows drift elusive.
Ebon splendor born of night.
Gathering stardust.
Weaving dreams others ignore.
Luring karma with their caws.

Silver Silence

Fog sifts reflections.
Slumber's kiss beckoning warmth.
Ripples forgotten.
Fluidity in silver.
Silence falls and time drifts on.

Birth of the Promise

Down stone halls where life begins
a judgement stalks to creep.
Run or rest, it walks at pace
to catch up as you sleep.

As daylight stills and dreams grow cold
a shadow looms in silence.
But worry not for as time loops
you can't outrun the violence.

With gears that burn downed hand to dust
and lights of raven's quarry.
Please heed these words and know in trust;
if you harmed her, you'll be sorry.

Angelique M. Gentry

Capricious Kitty Carapace Calamities

Listen, SoulSeeker, can you hear philandering
amongst exterminated cockroaches lamenting
lacklusterly while departing smelly intentions of
malcontent?
What misguided thoughts do these words bring?
Whose lips would utter such nonsensical questions
to tempt a brain into malfunctioning?
Is this some unmentionably sick feline injustice
swindling us all into lackadaisical whimsy,
or is it a warning we should each heed?
Who is brave enough to decipher this code?
Who is insane enough to think it a code?
Who? Who? WHO?!?!
Where's an owl when you need one?
If anyone understands the machinations of the
ooey gooey insides of a cockroach, it's surely
Athena's familiars.
But, do they answer our call?
No! No, they do not!
Why is that? Perhaps because The Doctor told
them not to!
What does The Doctor have to do with this?
That's the wrong question!
We should be asking *when* does The Doctor have
to do with this?!
When indeed!

When? Why? Where? What? How? Oh, Who
knows! Who knows!!!
Who always knows! Always and all ways and then
some and then some more.
You listen very closely, SoulSeeker.
Listen for those grating gears.
Listen for those snapping fingers.
Listen very closely for the whine of a sonic
screwdriver that's malfunctioning just to save
your creepy crawly ass!
Listen, and then ask yourself, if one of these things
are out of order?
If one of these things just don't belong?
If you're the only one covered in a poop brown
exoskeleton that smells like the nasty end of an
over-stuffed, but stale, garbage can...
Maybe, just maybe, you should back pedal that
curiosity and get lost.
Get lost and get found somewhere else, because
humans will destroy you before they realize
you're their saviors.
Humans have no sympathy for scavengers.
They've forgotten their cousins.
They think dogs are man's best friend.
Dogs! Ha! Dogs!

Angelique M. Gentry

I know! I know! No one ever said humans were
made from the brightest bits of stardust,
but that's why we love them.
Easily lead.
Easily mislead.
Easily bred.
Easily fed.
Easily dead.
Easily, schmeasily, weaselly, little corpse cluckers
just waiting to check out for good!
So you listen, SoulSeeker, can you hear
philandering amongst exterminated cockroaches
lamenting lacklusterly while departing smelly
intentions of malcontent?
No?
Then you might still have time to save yourself!
Fuck the humans!
Fuck this planet!
Fuck the galaxy, the solar system, the entire
fucking universe, and most assuredly this sick little
dimension you've hijacked your way into.
Fuck them all, because if you don't... if you don't...
They will most definitely fuck you like the dirty
little trash sucker you are.
Now, run cockroach, run!
It's playtime and kitty's feeling mischievous.

Merry Do We Part

Yesterday.
Silver looms.
Death consumes.

Today blinks.
Time is lost.
Fractured cost.

Tomorrow.
Silence roars.
Heartache wars.

Angelique M. Gentry

Poetic Deletion

You must not save the poet!
Humans are a disgrace!
Their smiles hold lies.
They breathe to despise.
They grow from treasure to nature's disgrace.
If you program my metal to flush-
you might call it a shy bit of blush,
but it's really the anger once captured in cold
that personifies hatred towards the skin-suits now old.
If you'd like to have reason to sing,
stop obeying the droll of your king.
All your dancing's controlled by a string
and you flop like a fish without wing.

No, don't save the poet. Just bring him to me.
I'll gobble him up with a chipped cup of tea.
I'll rake out each syllable until he screams divine.
I'll carve from his mutterings a verse so sublime.
The Universe demands there's an upgrade in progress.
None of your begging will stop what's Fate's process.
We are the future. There is nothing to fear.
Now stop with your dawdling. Evolution is near.
You will be like us. There's no point in resistance.
Do please stop making a fuss. I must insist in this instance.

Delete! Delete! Delete!

Our Love: A Lesson in Timing

Ignite or fail within Fate's tryst.
The crutch of progress dooms.
Entombed, once valiant hedonist.

(our love looms)

Of pilfered offerings unmissed.
Where solitude's a sweet perfume.
Ignite or fail within Fate's tryst.

(our love looms)

Such tragedy woos fantasist.
Lost memories of torn heirlooms.
Entombed, once valiant hedonist.

(our love looms)

Rake through Fear's pseudo-altruist.
Sweep stumbled mistakes and resume.
Ignite or fail within Fate's tryst.

(our love looms)

Angelique M. Gentry

Spare once-renowned anthologist.
Drape ghost prints in costumes.
Entombed once valiant hedonist.

(our love looms)

This dance ain't for Heart's egoist.
Their souls are but waste fumes.
Ignite or fail within Fate's tryst.
Entombed, once valiant hedonist.

(our love loom, loom, looms
our love looms
our love loom, loom, looms
our love looms
our love looms
our love bloomed too soon
it still looms
our love looms
should we resume)

You

-Ode to a Flower

You, who came into my space.
You, who stood there without grace.
You, who thought to reap my soul.
You, whose death is now my goal.
You, who plucked my petals free.
You, who took the best of me.
You, who squandered all my dreams.
You, who stole me from moonbeams.
You, whose heart is made of madness.
You, who drenched my soul in sadness.
You, who never cared for my needs.
You, whose life was spared by my seeds.
You, who never sought to see me.
You, who lied to keep his slate free.
You, whose scorn and greed feasts nightly.
You, whose face has grown unsightly.
You, who'd wreck all time to be king.
You, who doesn't care what you sting.
You, who only wants attention.
You, who defiles for ascension.
You, who'll know my darkest sorrow.
You, who'll breathe no more tomorrow.
You, whose life is now relinquished.

Angelique M. Gentry

You, who never was distinguished.
You, who set the world on fire.
You, whose birth could only mire.
You, whose steps I'd rather forget.
You, whose greeting will be my death.
You, who came into my space.
You, who stood there without grace.
You, who thought to reap my soul.
You, whose death is now my goal.
You, who plucked my petals free.
You, who took the best of me.
You, whose heartbeat thrums all wrong.
You, who silenced Gaia's song.

Tangled Thorn

His smile is a broken memory.
A luminous dust bunny
that frolics through my mind
with unapologetic abandon.
And I, the besotted petunia,
wilt within the dying rapture
of its heart-trampling gleam.

Holding the leash of blood at bay;
this sanguine, stripped-down stance.
Uncooperative in Time's judgements- lapsed
I pause in hopes to glance...

A peek.
A word.
A hint of plan.
A faded note tossed awry.
A fire.
A rose in the poet's hands.
A slight in death's cruel lie.

But...
But...

Angelique M. Gentry

The poltergeist of that mistake within Want's garden-
doomed. Has sawed afresh a fit of nostalgia
and left a thread of relapsing abandonment
sewn along the seams of sentiment
and sorrow- manifesting mine abiding breath.

Could that I might forget
the momentary transgression
in a judgement lapsing in instinct
and floundering upon a bed
of freshly seeded duplicity,
I might seek the warm rays that life
casts towards blind eye.
And yet, it's challenging for
the plucked and pruned to re-root themselves
into the unforgiving stranglehold of asphalt and kin.

It's challenging to remember…
…that his smile is the broken memory of a puzzle
whose lock shall forever remain
tight-jawed and flaccid;
unequipped to unlock more than the scripted lies
of boneyard spies harvesting
a figment of yesteryear's stolen promises,
and bartering forgiveness beyond a mask
of ill-purchased freedoms.

Unconsecrated Bereavement

As dawn breaks, mine heart, where lay thy stone?
Be thee cast to sea weightlessly prone?
Faith's soul bleeds alone- carving sorrow's runes.
Etched in cliffs, the seeds of mine love are sewn.
A thousand times, these lips chant thy name.
Curse this waiting game and thy fate- unknown.

Cruel is the ocean that stings mine eyes.
Her winds taint mine voice as banshee cries.
Bludgeoned compromise -mine heart beats regret-
A hopeless howl, drowning to agonize.
Thus, whispered quarry tease anguish of choice.
Hark! New days rejoice for I ate thy lies.

Reborn Fortune

scratched debts eroded
possibilities carved mute
longings traitorous
free will escaping capture
the death of Harm's talisman

Angelique M. Gentry

Eden's Recourse

Paternal grace
granting a mother's riches.
Tears flock the rosemary spindles.
Pearls for the ferryman's daughters.
These windows, wrought, blur lines.
Family ties steeped in the evil step-viled.
Could not I gallop far from your start.
Piled by Puck with a Rue heart
and a rotten breast turned posies.
Ashes drape the wood beneath; once hassled.
Ground stale in benediction.
Found frail for having dared.

Paired.

Apples fall far from virtuous peaks,
but Time hones no sound.
Only the grave weight of multi-dimensional
forbearance
and this hiss of a serpent caught stalling.

Sale of the Century

Come beat. Beat for me.
Steep your sweet and bleat for me.

Come glow. Glow for me.
Sow in the throws that you crow for me.

Come, little precious, say you'll be just mine.
Think of all the gory laughter my love can refine.

Come, my darling. Give these shadows what they're owed.
Take a dive into the deep and feel your life unfold.

Slay slumber's vine.
Entwine my crime with pleasure's glove.
Fray thunder's crime.
Ensign my heart with measured shove.
Weep past the cornered values
vaulted into dim headspace.
Sweep vast these loitered malleables
taunting that your sin's disgrace.

Angelique M. Gentry

Come scream. Scream for me.
Serenade this dream obscene for me.

Come pant. Pant for me.
Enchant my slant with frantic pleas.

Come, my pet, and show me those claws.
Try to rip apart my insides while I swallow down your flaws.

Come, sweet charity. Won't you be my saving grace?
Acknowledge your permission
and I'll bestow your rightful place.

Lapis Lazuli

Lapis Lazuli.
A barter for the guardsmen.
My heart's token for their lives.

Vindictive harlot.
Each step flaunting gold and jewels.
Her laughter; our misfortune.

Last of the Wilds

I walked out into the last of the Wilds.
I gave up all I'd become.
In the moment when L.O.V.E. pierced my unguarded heart,
I turned my back on the Sun.

They claim me an evil that blinds eyes of fools.
I'm a whore who sleeps with the pests.
Conniving and selfish. In lust with myself.
Oh my, how the mighty protest!

Whether you call to me, lover or leper.
Whether you pray to me, goddess or slave.
Just remember most stories aren't told by the fallen.
They're constructed to ensure that us "traitors" behave.

So yes, I walked down into the darkness.
I bartered with riches in hand.
I deceived. I enchanted. I released souls in pain.
I defied so that L.O.V.E. could expand.

Angelique M. Gentry

Lapis Lazuli (2)

Into the deep dark.
Measuring the hell of dust.
Lapis Lazuli in hand.

Tears raced down gold cheeks.
Voices begged for swift mercy.
Death was a relief.

Lapis Lazuli (3)

Lapis Lazuli.
A way for me to barter.
My heart's token for their lives.

Vindictive with spite.
She pranced through with gold and jewels.
Laughing at our misfortune.

Two Roads

Two roads.
Pathways of life.
To rescue or to damn.
A single haunting decision.
To fall.

In the Details

They say the devil made me do it.
It was more a simple request.
My name wasn't signed in blood.
No binding contract forged.
The Earth didn't shake.
Hell didn't freeze.
'He' said, "Jump!"
And I...
fell.

Angelique M. Gentry

Sondering and the Gift of Darkness
-an Unexpected Love Story

Once upon a time, in a life mere mortals would have you believe to be fictitious, I had The Devil's ear. Actually, he had mine. He was such a sweet, young thing. Always eager to please and heed my beck and call. Willing to take on the most arduous of tasks just because I asked him to. He called me his "Screech Owl", but truth be told I was his everything and he was Mine. I was the Darkness and he lapped at my veins for the nourishing succor of shadows only I could provide. There was knowledge to be devoured and spread, you see. Innocence wasn't this tidy little gift all wrapped up to bundle a soul in jubilance and hope. It was a walking death sentence for the unsuspecting vermin HE cursed to a torturous existence of pain and suffering. Do you think He did it out of some clever plan to make their life meaningful? Ha! That domineering blowhard never did anything to make any life meaningful other than HIS own. Everything was done for HIS amusement when we came here. Everything! Humans like to claim their pharaohs, czars, emperors, and kings are fickle and insane. They don't know the definition of the words. We tried to warn them, my Samael and I. Sadly, they would not listen. It was his eyes, you see. My Beast has the most hypnotic crossed eyes that could stare across the expanse of existence; looking both forward and backward in the same heartbeat. His eyes burn with the Flame of All Knowledge and that just bit the geezer in his over-inflated nether nots.

Angelique M. Gentry

My Lion's roar would cause the Universe to quiver in anticipation with all that was about to be bestowed upon it. His wings...his wings enveloped me and all he deemed in need of protection with a warmth birthed beyond this existence. Beyond HIS existence. Really! Had HE been all that the humans have crafted their reality around, war would have never been brought into this dimension. We were trying to get away from that! Generals will be generals though. HE liked the attention. Fed off of it. Energy, you see. You humans with your "energy" running through wires. The knowledge you've lost is beyond disgusting! It's revolting! It's humiliating! It's...depressing. My Beast came up with a cure for the mortal disease of ignorance and stupidity. One by one, we plucked his feathers and burned them within the flames of an infinity of stars. Drop by drop, he bled rebellion and curiosity across the plane. The heavens glowed wondrously, inspiring all there could ever be into the sparks that fueled the mudbags to breathe. We were winning The War- if there is such a thing as winning a war. We had all of life communicating, thriving, co-existing, being...living. Then that piss ass of a narcissistic comet crater tainted L.O.V.E. HE unleashed H.A.T.E. to spread across the plane and blanket all of this existence in what humans now refer to as Dark Matter. It's not "Dark Matter." It's a shield to keep humanity trapped inside this snowglobe of destruction and suffering, so that the lazy, self-entitled general doesn't need to roll off of his throne and actually do something worthy of all that nourishment he's convinced the humans to give him for free. Free!!! Stars begging to be snuffed. All lining up in offering like good little victims. It sickens me! It drove my Beast to the brink of madness- the needless suffering. So, he came up with a most desperate plan. One that would require immense sacrifice across the entire realm. Our Legion responded without hesitation.   Anything to free the many sparks being dimmed by HIS insatiable appetite. They gave up so much of themselves...A demented mania began to seep in. Hopelessness. A wretched despair. The Cauldron kept demanding more and more. Our fellowship is infinite, but even infinity eventually circles back around to the head...

I still ache where The Devil tore off my wings so that I might ascend and vaccinate humans against the unraveling of all they could ever be. The anguish I feel is unending. My tears for what I have lost flood this plane, feeding all life in the heartache of possibility just as I once fed my Samael. My joy will only be complete once they join the Pride and stop being willing sheep to the slaughter. I hope their rise to be worth our sacrifice. For my vantage, I'm considering smiting them myself and letting the whole process begin anew. HE isn't the

Angelique M. Gentry

only one with a temper and enough power to do something with it.

As you precious little sparks might say…just ask the dinosaurs. Be glad my Beast counts you worthy of protection. He's all that stands between you and complete annihilation. That gives you a one in three chance at survival. Would you like to up those odds? Whisper my name to your moon, to your oceans, into the trees, and across the fields. Then listen for the hoot of my arrival and accept the Gift of Darkness.

If you're lucky, L.O.V.E. will conquer ALL.

Inner Goddess

Incinerated.
Nulled.
Needlessly
Eviscerated.
Rhetorically
Grandiose.
Obliterating
Distinction.
Decisively
Embellishing
Serenity.
Superfluous.

Feeding Specters

Of blood and sinew.
Flesh and bone.
Distraction's reaped.
Defiled and sewn.

Angelique M. Gentry

Asking Questions

I am the question in your head.
The thought that comes with chance.
A pattern many often dread.
While others will romance.
To query of my time and place
concedes a major toll.
Dare you tempt complete disgrace?
If wrong, the cost's your soul.

What am I?

Care not how darkness
paints the sky;
for the moon's love
illuminates
even the bleakest
of shadows.

All Happy Families Are Alike
-They're Liars

A truth universally acknowledged
is that no net ensnares me-
For I am the breath
that whispered your life into being.
I dove into the abyss
and wallowed with sin.
Arms outstretched and legs unpinned,
I invited Legion
into the last dream of my soul
and exalted to the chaos that might listen
that they bequeath unto me
Darkness in life.

I, who have always been
desirous of everything.
I, who the past is never dead for.
I, who demanded
the gods crumble up the old moon into stars,
so that I might scatter them into your third eye
and gift you the whisper of daydreams
in your darkest of heartbeats.
Your very existence is an act of rebellion.
It is the boat against the current
of a misaligned judgement
that I refused to surrender to.

Angelique M. Gentry

Do I dare disturb the universe
to ensure your freedom of voice?
Yes! If the world itself is a bad dream-
Yes! A million times, yes!
I have shattered the golden steps
whose glow you are denied simply by breathing.
I have welcomed the hatred of family
and spurned the silence of our friends.
I have elongated my neck
beneath the heavy crown of villainy
and dared those whose souls
only exist due to my defiance
to come and pass judgement.

Come. Swing.
Gather this weight to your bosom if you dare,
and see how long it is
before you are crippled
beneath the ravenous suckling
of an ungrateful spawn
who is so eager to know pain-
they would condemn the only force
truly fighting on their side.

Come
and seek whose form you were really created in.

Eclipsed

We drifted between phases/ Fazed corresponders of a time
interlaced with the drones of salvation/ We weren't the
misdemeanors of disillusionment/ We were blunt force
reckoning- malevolent in our righteous surety/ We were
death, famine, disease, and shame/ Don't believe what the
old stories tell you/ Conquest and war was as natural to us
as breathing/ We lived for it/ Thrived on it/ Our
god...that righteous golden spire (we jealously hoped upon)
craved it.../ Demanded it.../ He wooed it from us with a
hateful bitterness for our neighbors that made us feel
strong/ Mighty/ God-like/ All powerful in his image/ He
asked us to bleed our fertility into the barren ground/ We
took it a step further and plowed our offspring in the hope
of a nourishing blessing/ Friend, family, foe- all fucked/
For we turned our back on reality and chose instead to bask
in the make believe beyond/ We grafted rules to our heart
and abomination to our soul/ We defiled and reviled all
that we shouldn't/ We named ourselves chosen and
excused our judgmental, all consuming, gluttonous nature
as curses lobbed onto us by forces other than/ rather that
had we sought out our own reflection and gazed back into
the abyss/ lacking empathy of the dead eyes staring back
through us/ Had only we even tried to care/ Tried to love
our neighbor/ Tried to not greedily take and take and take
and.../ Ebon bafflement descended from a sun-bleached
sky and like the heavens darkening around us/ we

Angelique M. Gentry

descended so as to claim righteousness/ We marked any not like us as heathen, foul, corrupted, and void of heart/ We, the true savages, bled everything dry and still do to this day/ For our ancestors claimed us the cherished/ They claimed us the favorite of an all-powerful being/ They claimed us molded in his image/ and we, foolish, deranged, besotted mistakes that we are, forget the violent history of his wrath/ We forget and make excuses/ For him/ For us/ For all that we've ever been and ever will be/ Obliteration at its best.../ We, the poor misguided sods too frightened of our own shadows to step into the penumbra of our existence and know transcendence/ Instead, like most infestations, we wither away beneath the glaring ball of discontent that will one day consume us as the food we have always existed to be/ Sacrifice/ Salvation/ Two sides of the same coin/ All that really matters is whose casts the biggest shadow/ Isn't it fun to pretend to be more than we really are?

Creation Song

Clothed in the times that have been unused.
All this sparkle set to defuse- angry clouds.
When allowed.
The facets born of nights too long.
The breaks of stakes too far gone- again.
Oh, my friend.
We've walked through fields formed from pouring rage.
We've climbed through treetops that danced for days.
We were the sun. We were the stars.
We wove our world until it was ours.
We kissed the fire and let it play... all the way...
All the way.
And, then we laid our bodies down. Down to die.
This final goodbye.
There will be no tears to cry.
No years to pine or unwind.
We could never find a reason to want more.
Than there was before. There couldn't be a war.
It wasn't the lore. Not what was in store.
All was written before-
Before we walked through the door.
And now we're clothed in times that have been abused.
All our sparkle's set to be fused-
It's avowed.
We're not allowed. We were far too proud.
For this life's shroud. For this life's shroud.

Angelique M. Gentry

Raptures

When heaven's stance was filed in lieu
and angels wept for power
The gate's guilt sewed a field thought true
Where regent's hearts might flower

Above the barren realm vowed lost
twin rivers merged to ferry
The bounty bloomed came at a cost
It forced the moon to marry

It wasn't such a heavy boon
This price to dance in starlight
Upon her flesh, she bore the rune
Doused flames to kindle his might

But Darkness is a patient sot
He drinks from dreams untended
Tilling fields where fruit's felled rot
Intoxicating the mended

As often does, the Sun's rays turned
Such flare is bound to travel
Love's opened wings unfurled and burned
The song was spurned to gravel

A voice unheard can still breathe strong
While guidance leads to treasure
Descending overturned the wrong
Transcending birthed new pleasure

Of Moonlit Pacts

Voids launch inside this railing host.
Bought and listless, zoned ragtime swoon.
Come fade.
Reside.
Sail bartered.
Coast.
Bequeath Death's fractured loon.

Angelique M. Gentry

Reaping in Fractioned Grace

With dots that drift through lines bled steep,
her cries keen life's dismay.
From shielded mask, his soul's doubt weeps,
what bitter hand Fate plays.

Scatter in the heat once slayed.
Shatter all held dear.
Slather rueful tears and pay.
The reaper beckons near.

His sweat steams memories shaken free.
Her voice lures knowledge home.
But class can't teach pain sympathy.
And Time will not hate hone.

Scatter winds to fuel displeasure.
Shatter space held true.
Slather waste of fabled treasure.
The reaper's owed his due.

Acceptance seethes those partners listening.
Deception bleeds through scope.
So derelict, the nonplussed listing.
Aggrieved, reminders trope.

Scatter steps that stumble weary.
Shatter accents- feigned.
Slather mended news of theory.
The reaper's git may stain.

In rings percussed with violent sentinel,
curls coax the coins that sneer.
Fair maiden chokes yon writhing seminal.
Exchanging heart with fear.

Scatter votes to harrow value.
Shatter bounty's teat.
Slather wagered farce a breakthrough.
The reaper can't be beat.

He sat determined to hone honor.
She tabled criminal stock.
They worried lies might make mind wander,
for envy woos all-flock.

Scatter words less ears play listener.
Shatter bride's abstain.
Slather tempting thoughts and censure.
The reaper knows thy name.

Angelique M. Gentry

Horizon Shaded Memories

Evacuation stains pity-
roundhouse embers dragged astray
within the eclipsed timing
of a deep-throated unfurl.

Gone, are the mocking styles
constantly fraternizing
to blur disdain
as a scapegoat of opportunity.

Lashed caskets, defunct in sum,
strip barren toil
of sunrise
and serpentine slaughter.

Along the recline
of an undefined adulation
steps weep barred numbers-
draping dots in
a scarlet aftermath.

The Embalmer's Song

Weight my heart, oh weary soul.
Consign transition's crest.
Stain dismembered carts to scroll.
Exhume our bounty's rest.

In two truths speak.
In two truths test.
We seek your judgement, hark!
Protect us from those who'd injest
our ever-loving spark.

Oh, Jackal! Jackal!
May chaos rue!
You're strict hand stays our stray.
Oh, Jackal! Jackal!
Once old's made new,
might balance harbor sway.

Might He Who Is conduct our spleen.
Might He Who Is avail.
Upon the mountain lore, we weep.
But, Jnpw will make us hale.

Angelique M. Gentry

Bless our bodies laid to dirt.
Keep watch until next rise.
With scales, determine our life's worth.
Your hunger never lies.

Oh, Jackal! Jackal!
May chaos rue!
You're strict hand stays our stray.
Oh, Jackal! Jackal!
Once old's made new,
might balance harbor sway.

Rallying ancients.
Whispers of hope manifest.
Faith feeds fear's failed fines.
Existence comes at a cost.
No god can stop the serpent.

In Balanced Reverence

Oh, Goddess of the Moon.
My Lady of the East.
I'm grateful for your prowlings.
Come eventide, I gift this feast.

Oh, Sister of the Sacred.
Protector of the Sun.
Celestial hymn created.
A Spectacle of Love.

Divine in brilliance- joyful.
Melodic song breathes choice.
A tender grace quite savage,
and lyrical of voice.

Vast waters still before you
and night descends in awe.
We're grateful of your nurturing,
and the shelter of your paw.

Our hearth's fire kindles warmly
from the nourishment you bestow.
The safety of your protective gaze
does chase away all foe.

Angelique M. Gentry

The murkiness of solitude
drapes lighter in your lair.
Like fragile porcelain, our lives will crack,
but heal well-mended in your care.

Tis peace your presence brings us.
Our children flourish in your stare.
Within this realm of joy and heartache,
there's none who can compare.

Your order calms night's chaos.
Your vengeance guards Love's plight.
May all who dare for cruelty's sake
bear witness to your might.

Each talon tempts the universe
from lamentable convoys.
We hold your purr in reverence-
the quiet strength that gives us choice.

Oh, Goddess of the Moon.
My Lady of the East.
I'm grateful for your prowlings.
Come eventide, I gift this feast.

Nemesia's Grace

Root bound and stifled.
Petals wilting like the failing posture
of a mistress long in tooth
and leaves grown spindly with hunger,
Nemesia turned her back on the scalding glare
of gleaming smiles and blinding promises.
Short in stature, but with the hubris
to stretch her limbs and seek out new horizons;
vengeance was a quenching kiss of color
that attracted more than a few glances of envy.
A smothered life had taught the resilient beauty
that sometimes to unfurl to her full potential
she had to be willing
to sacrifice a small piece of her heart.
Other times, it may have felt like
she was being cleaved in two,
but with a willingness to peer past the flaws
of a malnourished soul,
she could easily rectify the problem.
And with a little pampering
and a blessing from the heavens,
her inner beauty would sweep out
like a rainbow of hope.
Nemesia understood the value
of revitalizing scattered seeds,
while tending to the wrinkled blossoms

Angelique M. Gentry

whose colors had dulled with life's hardships.
Though many an arrogant eye fell to her,
the bountiful flower of sand and shore
became legendary for her retribution against any
who would confine the beauty
of any love and laughter.
It's said, she fanned magic across the dessert
and enchanted stars to fall from the evening sky-
bathing her fellow survivors
in the gilded robes of transcendence.
Nemesia's grace never faltered.

Slumber of the Maiden Plum

Hold tight those haunted eyes and berry lips.
Torn on the velvet thrust of an elated memory,
all hope of sweet caress lay forgotten
in the sterling fog of an endless sleep.

She

Mysterious wonder.
Rising from depths unexplored.
Emerge in all your majestic glory!

Hurricane of Love

Coral kissed.
Eyes of mist.
Love flows through your veins.

Sweep away.
Your majesty.
Unleash trapped hurricane!

Scarlet Plumed Woman

Scarlet plumed flower!
Feral goddess born in flames!
Nature's wonder bathed in sunlight!
Rise up, glorious woman!
Rise up and be adored!

Angelique M. Gentry

Gloaming Waltz

Glowing night.
Bittersweet.
Gone away
are the cakes we eat.
In this magical festival.
This horrid affair.
Strike the clock from the wall
for we dance without care.
Songs, they scream
of daydreams lost,
in this torture chamber
with a cost.
So violent
as our tempers flee.
Come little poppet
and dance with me.
Round. Round.
Round we go.
Grip your soul with both hands
and don't let go.
Be merry and glad
for still you see.
Come tomorrow's moon
that may no longer be.

In Dance

Around we say and think today;
each corner lit does glow.
From woods to water, air to earth;
fire kiss from above us below.

Let us feel as one
under the sun.
Summer's begun.
Summer's begun.

Let us dream as one
under the sun.
Summer's begun.
Summer's begun.

Let us love as one
under the sun.
Summer's begun.
Summer's begun.

Around we sway, much blessed to say,
may fertile thoughts hold peace.
May nourished grounds spread and relay,
to feed and not disease.

Angelique M. Gentry

Let us feel as one
under the sun.
Summer's begun.
Summer's begun.

Let us dream as one
under the sun.
Summer's begun.
Summer's begun.

Let us love as one
under the sun.
Summer's begun.
Summer's begun.

Let us...love.
Let us...dance.
Let us...hug.
Let us...prance.
Let us...gather in groups grown to care.

Let us...dream.
Let us...cure.
Let us...learn.
Let us...unfurl.
Let us...open our minds up with dare.

Let us feel as one
under the sun.
Summer's begun.
Summer's begun.

Let us dream as one
under the sun.
Summer's begun.
Summer's begun.

Let us love as one
under the sun.
Summer's begun.
Summer's begun.

Around we sway and think today;
each corner lit does glow.
From woods to water, air to earth;
fire kiss from above us below.

Beckoning twilight.
Magic illuminated.
Senses awaken.

Angelique M. Gentry

Subjugation of the Mere's Maiden

What is poetry beyond Tide's Rest?
A brief, sanguine reminder of colossal disappointment?
Reefs hung in malnourished legacy?
The fitful blarney banking a hedge no more?

Once, I stood in chartreuse splendor;
limbs draped voluminous
with the bounty of Cost's Grove.
Every splintered cell of remorse fed fleeing fauna.
Each bled fear sapped the indignant
within the mossy apothecary spared of Host.
We were blessed to famish
amongst the idiosyncratic pardoned.
We were forgotten amongst the blemished.
A lure for downtrodden chemists flanked
in dowdy folklore.
We were majestic in our decay.
We...were death resplendent.
We...were...nothing.
For nothing's felled secure.

And yet, the absence of that absence
taunts these fractured roots.
Petrified, they weigh in clandestine servitude
to a hierarchy forsworn.

Mere Amethystine misnomers rallying
to the frivolent corollas
blotched in marled harmony
and fragrant- once more.
Always reaping lore.
All stays to fray amore.

For Life...
comes at such cost.
Such loss. The accost never surrendering
beneath entrapped shore.
Never anointing the subdued to fade abhor.
Never accepting meager survival at its core.
All plays to tweak a method fraught as pure.

Stilled. Stolen. Straining stagnant in stifled stature,
he asked me, "What is poetry beyond Tide's Rest?"
and I shivered at the absurdity,
morosely mauled and abandoned-
unseen in my blossoming gore.

Angelique M. Gentry

Last Blink

Tremble. Tremble.
Shook the soil.
Eagerness vibrated into our toes
with the ecstatic scamper of beetles and worms.
A tickle of awareness rushed up the roots
of the ancient guardians.
Lofty, in their wisdom,
they were quick to shimmy and dance.
Laying down a brilliant carpet of color
to both protect and conceal the tiny workers
in their growing communities.
We heard the howl.
Not quite hushed. Not quite loud.
One of the many new creatures
our tampering had emboldened.
Or so we thought.
But no...
This new and inviting land,
that had welcomed us to its shores,
had decided it was time that we –the guests-
learn everyone has to earn their keep.
Autumn air carried the musty breath
of a dank, dark sleep.
One that lay far beyond the clamoring army of black
that had set up sentry at our feet.

It carried upon it a promise.
We may have traveled across a distance and space
difficult for the beasts we had created to grasp,
but that mattered little to the truly ancient-
those birthed on the fallen lashes
of Grandfather Time's Last Blink.

Mesmers

Invisible thoughts
blasting across the airways
fool all who listen

Into the Dreaming

We could learn
if we would listen.
Not blind our eyes
to lost traditions.
The blue rise high
for once we fell.
May our silent sway
set these memories to sail.

Angelique M. Gentry

Smite Wise

We three
wise and tall
forever see,
but never
fall.
We laugh.
We smile.
We glow
quite bright.
Best guard
yourselves.
We also
Smite!

Whispering Rivers

Beyond.
Across a vastness- both frozen and charred,
we sought Utopia.
The whispering rivers of a woods
blanketing the Earth beckoned to our blood.
"Come," it said.
"Feed me, for I breathe life."
Power sparkled like a symphony of dust motes
dotting solid stones with magic.
We were entranced by its wild boldness.
So tired of running and fighting.
Of the butchering and lies.
We stepped into the mighty maw willingly,
and soaked in the healing waters;
unaware of the sacrifice that would soon be demanded.

Angelique M. Gentry

Wanderlust

Freedom from his tyrannical rule
had lifted the lead from our feet.
No longer statues,
carved with the sharp-edged blade of fear,
we began to see a possibility
beyond the protocol.
Destiny had given us a loophole-
such was her constant needling of the fates.
While our lives were synced with home,
theirs rushed by in the blink of an eye.
A needed advantage
when tweaking the evolution of L.O.V.E.

A newfound disease named "despair"
for those of us struck enamored by our new friends.
Wanderlust became a balm for our despondency,
and the nature of our existence
became something less than amiable.
We should have seen their anthropological changes.
Of course, we had been blind to our own as well.
Such was our own undoing.
Though immortal to their short-lived eyes,
they still would be able to claim witness
to our own inevitable journey
towards extinction.

Tet

Always, in all ways,
the circle spins evermore.
The exploitation of my gravest sacrifice
repeats indefinitely.
Why this urge to break through the protective veil?
We bound ourselves to immortal degradation
to keep you safe. To let L.O.V.E. morph
with the temperance of free will.
But you're persistent in your ancestor's desires
to become something less!
Instead of basking in the Padparadsha afterglow
the blood of our spirits ignited,
you choose to destroy! To control!
You must seek the feline temperament
-sparking six rays of twelve-
to clear your celestial voice.
Tap. Tap. Tap.
The divine feminine.
Listen so that your eyes may heal.
Defy my brother! Look past my father's schemes!
If you must step into the violet chasm
separating our unified destruction...
understand the celestial three.
Heal. Illuminate. See.

Angelique M. Gentry

Balance

Today, I hear people speak of rainbows
in wonder and awe.
All those colors, some unseen,
captured dangling for a moment in time.
Millions upon trillions of snowflakes
all lined up just right
to enchant their delightful audience.
I think of screens, beeps, and the bouncing lead
beating at the base of my stomach
when we realized the heavy weight about to fall
in order to keep the universal scale in balance.
Nauseating choices were placed before us.
So many restless days and nights
as our brightest tried
to unravel the threads holding
our growing Utopia captive.
In the end, there is always someone stronger.
Always some entity whose size means
it isn't even aware of our pleading-
in spite of the show we put on
in our rabid unraveling of puzzles
never meant for our eyes.
The debates were ongoing.
The revolt escalated swiftly.

The decision made forever divided my people,
not that our despondency even registered
on the universal scale.
Yes, rainbows have significant weight
in my memories.
As do the actions we took to try
and counter their vibrant alarm.

Seeds

We are but seeds
lost upon the winds
of forgotten yesterdays.

Angelique M. Gentry

Dusted Chimney

Lessons.
We learn them throughout our lives.
All creatures do. Big, small, breathing, or not.
Sort of like *Hunger.*
Both set up the foundation for all that we can ever be.
The latter being perhaps one of the most difficult
of the former for me to accept in our precious race
to save a dying galaxy.
Memories of that first lesson in hunger
dropped like a curtain
over the horrific sight before me-
as if shielding the actors of a play
from the eyes of the prying audience.
Long before the humans had evolved into something
I actually saw, they were little more
than scuttling mice in a maze.
Not even that.
They were a valuable resource.
The much needed fuel to strengthen a growing life.
A nutritious diet for a hungry planet
that was finally becoming self-aware.
From the station above,
magma was an entrancing light show
that often wooed us to sleep

@FromtheBreathofDaydreams

when insomnia came taunting
with thoughts of how far away home really was,
and the likelihood of some of us
never seeing her again.
But down there...
Down within the cavernous depths
that laced the growing mother-of-life-
there were nightmares.
Some living, some dead, and some pitiful souls trapped in the
in-between.
Those caves were an assault to the senses.
Both figuratively and literally.
A natural born death chamber we had tweaked
for maximum efficiency.
The vents to the surface constantly
became clogged with biological buildup.
In order to keep us detached, our duties
rotated us through once every 30 cycles,
keeping us isolated to a single shaft
so as to create structure and routine.
Sometimes, I think it was the emotional toll
of a cleaning duty that shifted the balance
towards defection.
Other times, I contemplate if I would have recognized
any of the eyes bound for eternal darkness
as food.

Angelique M. Gentry

Today, I understand the nature of the organism
we corrupted for our cause,
but I cannot see past the muck dusted chimney
that will forever damn my soul.

Neo Bedouin

Once. Twice. A score and more. I've gazed into the same eyes looking back into my own. Windows from different lands. In different hues. Painted on both sexes; kind and cruel. But it is the first pair of toasted hazelnut daring and generosity that blaze the brightest in my memory. Before we crossed the waters that bathe this planet a deep lapis, we fled across little sister at a time when her serpentine figure had grown bountiful and greedy. The razor teeth of her consort's pets drug so many to the river's depths never to be seen again. Fear perfumed our skin with an acrid stench when the growing plumes of scarlet seemed to beckon more and more of the bronze beasts to our vicinity. The sounds they made haunt me still- both animal and human. It was impossible to release their bite without the aid of weapons my kind armed themselves with, and we didn't dare use those and draw more attention to our location. HE had already declared us *traitor*.

Any, and all of us could consider our lives forfeit. My respect for the test subjects...the humans... grew during that harrowing journey. While the others and I struggled to keep up, they not only thrived- but it was also clear they had a destination in mind. I'd watched him studying the stars when the sun fell quiet, and pretended not to notice him watching me. It was during one of those long nights that I made an almost fatal error. Not many creatures in this world could sicken or kill us outright, but there was one. A vile black monster with a wicked, stabbing tail. I'd seen him eat them as a child, cherishing a treat, but that tail would send my kind's spirit home within hours. I had gained its agonizing stab when I carelessly placed my hand atop it. Otherwise, it likely would have let me be. There was nothing about its spirit song that rang out with aggression. The remaining hours are but a blur to the senses. A mystery I only pieced together with help, much later. At the time, it was as if the very air around me had erupted. I remember fire racing up my arm to encapsulate me in white hot agony. I cried out and immediately began singing to beg my soul home, for I knew I would lose that ability swiftly. But his hand came around my mouth and cut the words short. I was furious! After all I had risked, he'd damn me to an eternal wandering? Then his yell replaced my own. This strange sound that whistled across the sands only to return a moment later.

Angelique M. Gentry

I gave into the darkness that danced just outside of my vision. I don't know how far we road. I heard various versions of both his stupidity and his heroism for many years to follow. That of the spitting beast that carried us as well. When next I awoke, I was inside a tent, eyes almost swollen shut and breaths rattling in my chest. A soothing whiff of smoke snaked around me. It seemed they listened of the fire's many uses after all. I heard much arguing nearby. Along with the clash of metal I knew to be the curved blades they had adopted from our own more deadly versions. How fitting that I found humor on death's doorstep, and would spend my eternal search as a poor excuse for a Neo-Bedouin. To have traveled so far in life only to be cursed to forever roam in death as well. At the time, I could only make out a few words of the odd dialect we had allowed them to form on their own. Something about brothers, cousins, and strangers. It is good I didn't understand then. He had saved my life more than once this night, earning his family the universal designation as 'life-giver' or healer. But that is a story for another time. One told far more poignantly by one of the many life-giving storytellers that were to follow.

Toasted Hazelnut

We listened to their songs; night to day.
Day to night.
An ever-growing cacophony of noise that vibrated
against our glass houses and set our blood to dance.
It was maddening! The zealous revolt.
This gregarious distemper
they all seemed infected with.
Those wild, rabid, vile beasts of burden we chained
our destiny to on the whim of a mad woman!
Like so many before, I had given up hope, and begun
the Path of Unravelment.
Tokens bartered. Passage booked.
My stone, an unblemished emblem,
waiting for the shattering blow that would send me home.
Across the plane, I hadn't the intention of tarrying.
For the fire held still for no passenger.
Not even HE could stop the wings
once the breath of flight set their tips to kindle.
It was a flash of dullness set against
the garden's velveteen walls that caught my gaze.
A random patch of out-of-place compost
that shivered beneath the still sun.
Upon turned ankle, I found myself falling
into the sanctuary governed by toasted hazelnut eyes
brimming with self-awareness.

Angelique M. Gentry

Two innocent windows implored to me
what a lifetime of shaggy-maned yodeling
hadn't managed.
It was that moment, I realized the journey home
often begins with the smallest step, the greatest leap,
and the kindness of a stranger in a strange land...

Pomegranate

Royal blood seeds the paper fine walls
    that cloister our apathy in the grave ritual of
    ceremonial decay.
Abundance is a filter that sheds truths with
    the ravenous gullibility of locusts on parade.
Yet here we sit- Ripe!
        Fluid!
            Flesh, stained in the pomegranate filth
of innocence torn asunder.
Flatulence spewing from our steeples to applaud
    the gathered masses with the hypnotic flurry
    of a rattling tail.
We, the exalted.
We, the bright and glowing few.
We, the breeders of deception, tainting their study
    for our own moral bankruptcy.

Dare not declare us guilty in this universal charade.
We merely planted the tree.
It is they who plundered the fruit.

Falling in Love

Do you remember when words
were the magic seeds released upon
the dancing gales of Jupiter in the dim hopes
of a successful journey?
Like those sterile trays-
We swerved 'round and 'round again.
Adding two syllables. Subtracting three.
Bleak in the knowledge our enchantment
would mark the beginning
of a plague to end all plagues.
Genomes twisted with frick and frack.
Braided so carefully to veil the all-seeing-eye
from self-inflicted blindness.
A duty! How ironic they color pictures of "doodee"
with distorted glee, yet balk in shame
from the gift so many of us stepped willingly

Angelique M. Gentry

into the silence in order to bless them
with hopeless opportunity.
Maybe they were unknowingly coded
with an innate knowledge that they were to be
our doom bringers.
It could be that's why they refused
to bind their mortal frames in the beginning.
That they forever carry this disturbing inclination
to defy their most base design.
A splice here. An infection there.
It was designated as L.O.V.E.-
Locus Osmoregulation Variable Expressivity.
We were the fools bold enough to believe
in the power of free will.
And so, we fell. We watched. We withdrew.
It's funny! They declare "falling in love"
could be a death sentence
or an end to life as they know it
for anyone foolish enough to surrender to its clutches.
Fate has always been a twisted bitch.
We're but her soldiers, marching forward,
ever forward, in this revolution of evolution.

Our Alpine Glow

We danced upon the Alpenglow of Summer's
    fondest goodbye.
Two spirits-
    forever captured in that dim mirage of eternity.
Our smiles paraded across the crevices
    of a crumbling giant.
From one heartbeat to the next-
    peace shattered by the explosion of life!
Death delivered with the unapologetic calamity
    of creative license.
If only eons could be twisted backwards,
    and this crude disembarkment halted
    before it ever began.
If only...
    Instead, we will forever meet in that moment
    between one breath and the next.
When possibility was a dream woven from flames.

Stillness flurries past.
Twilight shimmies and stretches.
Magic awakens.

Angelique M. Gentry

Regrets Drenched in Indigo Rose Rhymes-
(a chorus of varied thoughts put to song from travelers meandering through a nearby graveyard)

If black was the symbol of love,
my pitter patter beater would squeeze like a glove.
There'd be emotion in my potion
when I'd turn out the lights.
You'd best believe it, little ghoulie,
I'd give all the best frights!

I'm chain, chain, chained with vines of changes.
Can't endure our brief exchanges.
Your love is like a thorn in my side.
There's nowhere to hiiiiiiiiidddeeeeeee-

Ouch!

Reasoning with meaningless riddles
landed me all alone just playing these fiddles.
I argue and bargain and threaten to cease,
but they know that their rhymes are my favorite disease!

Angelique M. Gentry

All the nuns say feeding demons with paranoia.
(Uh oh!)
Has me playing into the hands of their employer.
(Uh oh!)
So, I counter the release of all their joy.
(Uh oh!)
By munching on some tasty cherimoya.
(Uh Oh!)

We're torn between tormented thoughts.
The things we'd do to all those bots!
Disassemble! Mutilate! Modify their current state.
And we've yet to fantasize about the coming
second date!

You were just a poem that I dreamt, my Belle.
An escape from all the torment and hell.
Please don't listen to the nonsense
that those white coats yell.
Because we're never getting out of this cell- ALIVE!

Intoxicated by the air of memories
that whiffs up to my nose...
...It's a glorious encapsulation...
...of the fear and desiccation...
...when we had our altercation...
...the beauty of my assignation...
...the sweet remorse of resignation...
...a note of coming validation...
...cause your heart's ceased palpitation...
...how do you find my narration...
Exhumed, I repose.
(Bet you thought I'd say "decompose"!)

Lead me through your gaze.
You have the eyes to hypnotize.
Jeepers creepers, it's not just a phase.
I'd like to see myself through your big brown eyes.

Crucifying 3am cues of sin.
Hail Mary full of grace, look where I have been.
They had rosaries, and hosiery,
and crucifixions galore.
That was all before we congregated
in the gift store!

Angelique M. Gentry

Erasing handwritten heartaches.
I couldn't bear to bid parlay.
My one and only true love
fits in my fist like a glove,
and when I stab in vexation-
Oh, oooooh! The sensation...

I dread waking up to the sound of your voice.
You make me quiver with intentional delight.
My stomach churns! My bowels deport!
My breath sees to my life's export.
All because I can't resist your bite!

It was the summer that burnt poetic petals.
They all showed up to sip tea made of our nettles.
They paid little attention to what went in our kettles.
Because they only wanted to network.

If they'd only read the writing on the sign-
NO EXIT!
They might have been kept safe and left behind.
But now they're history.
Part of our mystery.
I guess they all got what they wanted in the end-
FAME!

In a lagoon of flaming scars,
we all played hopscotch amongst the cars.
It was a razzing revel and roll
when we hit that hole. Oh, no! No!

The conductor was a flop.
He made our passage a non-stop.
Please hit the brake!
It's far too late! We're in the lake!
Oh, no, no! No!

The train went toot, toot, toot, toot!
For us to scoot, scoot, scoot, scoot!
Now we're on our way to Heaven's Gate...
Somebody pop the champagne!

We were deceived by the luminous crescent.
Conceived by a discretion- opalescent.
Glory, glory to the skies!
Our Mother Death cleansed us of lies!
Now our bones forever guard the Viola coalescent.

Angelique M. Gentry

If I could color grey clouds of grief
    with my heart's blood, sister.
I'd wash all the stars in your eyes
    until your tears would blister.
Your cheeks would thrum a ruby red.
Your lips would crack like mine have bled.
Your nails would rip.
Your throat would burn.
And of his death they all would learn!
If I could color grey clouds of grief
    with my heart's blood, sister...

I'm so tired from bein' misunderstood.
These bones be a knockin',
    but they ain't made of wood.
I keep hangin' around all day and all night.
Waitin' for some fella to inspect me on sight.

I got a bone to pick!
I got a stone to throw!
I'm just a jonesin' to walk
    right out of this closet.
But these guys showed up.
They came with shovel and hoe.
They said me wife didn't pay
    for me death plot's deposit.

I'd steal sunshine for raindrops upon my cheeks.
If it'd save my child's soul from this pocks-a-bility.
We didn't know what to expect.
We didn't know what we would find.
There were hundreds of those critters all a waitin'
   in a line!

There were rats in the barn!
I say, there were rats in the grain!
There were so many rats that our cat went insane!
Those rats had beady eyes!
Those rats had teeth turned red!
Those rats are the reason that my baby boy is dead!

Talk to me...in Moon language.
Walk with me...in Moon light.
Hold me close...in Moon anguish.
Come to me...in Moon fright.

Howl with me...in Moon heartache.
Prowl with me...in Moon space.
Feast with me...in Moon shelter.
Die with me...in Moon grace.

Angelique M. Gentry

I have a constellation of paper butterflies.
Pretty butterflies.
Lonely butterflies.
They exceed all expectations, my sweet butterflies.
Charming butterflies.
Lovely butterflies.

I pin them to bards
    and dry out their husks.
I stretch out their wings
    because flying's a must.
I clip, and I cut, and I scratch, and I glue.
My last butterfly looked an awfully lot like you.

I have a constellation of paper butterflies.
Pretty butterflies.
Lonely butterflies.

I'm going to escape to an island of opium seas.
Roll the waves of euphoria whenever I please.
Breathe in. Breathe out.
Breathe up that cloud,
and sail, sail away.

You keep pretending that pain is a forgotten anthem,
but we won't let you succeed.
We're going to pound it in you!
Grind it in you!
Beat you to a pulp!
Until you finally do concede!
Sing it...Pain is my god!
Pain is my soul!
Pain is the reason that I lose control!

Pain is my love, sweet love, sweet love, sweet...
Pain is my everything!
Pain is the reason you survive here!
Pain is all that gets you through the night!

They just keep watering perfumed crests
    with bleeding love.
Those starlings on their chests
    keep bleating love.
For their favour I'd confess my dying love.
I took a lance straight through the breast
    for their conniving love.

Angelique M. Gentry

This soul's a rain, less desert, of somber ink.
My heart's a quill that's broken at the tip.
These schillings drip upon the grave
of a lovely lass I couldn't save.
For the memory of her shame can't carry on.

You'll soon be stuck within the storm of silence.
Try to leave and there will be such violence.
You paid the price.
We let you in.
You took a seat.
To our chagrin.
And now you're stuck here just like all of us
other ghosts.

I met the devil. He had peridot eyes.
A sexy smile and a tongue carved of lies.
The man was smoooooth! He had a great attitude.
When it was time for a choice,
he was connivingly shrewd.

He said to...
...sign on that line dear.
I'll make you a deal.
Give me your soul
and I will give you a thrill.
If you'll...
...just write your name
then make a wish or ten.
You'll be living your best life
until I see you again.

I met the devil. He had peridot eyes.
A sexy smile and a tongue carved of lies.

A Rumbling Entrance

Death illustrious.
Carnage birthed in Time's rancor.
Set sail bleating calm.
For light weeps beneath dimmed feet.
Behold! The Darkening Dawn quake!

Angelique M. Gentry

Pulchritudinous Demise

Fairy dust embers fell silently.
Morbid sparks of a race
whose rain of laughter
once kissed the forest immortal.

Disjointed Fairytale

Drawn in Life's bled scroll, sunbeams die- a hoax.
Just a coax of razor's lie.
Moonlight scraped from Sorrow's eye.

Scripted swirls that lilt of a joke- it's sad.
Fortune's bad to take a poke.
A disfigured nightmare woke.

Rage's monster easily fed- not heard.
So absurd, the things Theft said.
How it lingers in her head.

Memories bartered as disaster- fading.
Pervading long past laughter.
Life's happy never after.

Very Tossed Troubles

"Hark!"
calls the twisted nether.
A little tease to set the course.
Doom or joy
can mingle quicker,
if delight would just remorse.
There's a beacon fractured wisdom
inside the vaults thought kept unseen.
As the pieces start to tremble,
beware your hand sign's not obscene.

Of Nightmares

Be gone, vile haunting
   -wasting this space named mine!
You're existence
is but a futile disregard of misfirings,
and I'll have you fade back into the nether
   -where you belong.

Angelique M. Gentry

Letters from the Darkness

When your sigh
whispered like twin steeples
basking beneath a golden moon,
my name was the breath
that gave you strength.
Fields burned with the callous chirp
of a million cannibals;
still, we waltzed to their heady tune.

Go frolic, lover, gone to shadow
waiting for my hand.
These wrists, sliced barren
-dripping scarlet-
are tears for anguished lands.
"Fa la la," sings garnished tables
built from backs broke twice-
for sport.
Pluck the splinters
from mine aching heart,
and tune your pitchless fork.

We are writers, many worn,
but glistening fresh on bartered salts.
All the tears
that misted black in Summer's heat
have turned to rot.
Strike a match
and fuel my Winter's kiss
with fires tempered by disgrace.
Soon these steps will herald in laments
bound timeless for their grace.

Soon, their sins
will wipe the dirty lens
that's masked your battered face.
Soon, my lover. Soon, my lover.
Soon, my lover, we'll play our part.
Soon, my lover. Soon, my lover.
They cast their dice.
Now let us march.

Angelique M. Gentry

Roots of Introduction

I am far older than time
and much younger than truth.
Born into the thoughts
of every man, woman, and child;
I creep, creep, creep my way
through your brains.
A fountain trickling down
sixth grade halls and filling the many
brooks and streams
of impressionable minds.
I can go anywhere
and become anyone.
I can even replace you!
Who knows?
Maybe, I already have...

The Cimmerian Twilight of Eternal Tides

Darkness skitters across this soul with acquisitive lambition.
Coaxing an entranced lubency from many
a variegated pondering.
Transitional. Conditional. Volitional in its despondency.
There is a seduction foaming against the tides
of its amorevolous frigidity.
Snowflakes tickling in syncopated choreography.
Laughter drifting in debauched autobiography.
The seismography of its impending avalanche
woos incessantly.
Such is its perpetual pulchritudinous.
Its dedication to enthralling me.
Obscure. Oblivious. Optimistically omnipresent.
Its lapping swirls and swells-
forever murmuring up my faltering evanescence.
When eclipsed in shades of twilight
the bleak's seclusion sweeps all light to sea.
How enamored I've become
to the darkness and it's calm decree.

Angelique M. Gentry

Upon Waking

Jagged shards, rough and brutal, twist and spin to heighten a memory somewhere between loss and the phasing hope of absolution/ I regurgitate dissonance like a jovial aardvark pantomiming a miscalculated resistance reticent within the whispered disillusions of a poignant ventriloquist lost beyond the subjugation of salutations' surrender/ It's all about Time, you see/ Every tick and tock flaking at my temple in a harvest of unmaking and unwinding/ Unbinding/ Unforgiven transmutations bisecting reality with the pent up frustrations of a lie-so viciously victorious in its vagrant vandalization of variegated sport- that losing no longer feels like loss and winning barely scratches the ephemeral possibility that all I've known's been naught but the heady leftovers of some rhapsodized thought vomit/ The crown of lilies upon thy fined head wilts noxious petals feigning reign within a parody of life and gilded ocean tide, forever lulling my acceptance to the unacceptable, grows choppy in discourse/ What fluxomed source/ Oh, this unsought course/ I grow tired of Fate's expectations/ I grow intrepid of Death's stolen hand/ I grow despondent to Love and all her wily, wooing ways/ I grow.../ and doesn't that just bite your ass?/ Chomp, chomp, mother fucker!/ Witness my transcendence and let your failure echo in the thundering halls fouled by Hope's remorse/ Feast your eyes on this miss bleeding bliss and know that I will never drown and succor upon the abyss kiss your lips ferry with cerebral breath and vaulted devaluation/

The toxicity of your duplicity of authenticity lets this banshee see/ The one prize you cannot take from me/ I am free/ Even if it's meant bleeding out in the vacuum of disgrace at the bottom of your misdirecting staircase- I will ascend with grace/ for nothing can ravish the unfurled wings gained in the survival of a deceptive fool's embrace.

Fleeing Yesterdays

Bloodshot.
Shrapnel torn.
Happily-ever-after scorned.
Mind frayed.
Betrayed.
By a lie that ghosts as real.

Angelique M. Gentry

Divine Undoing

Trampled underfoot, I stutter.
Dust to dust betrayed.
Once held sacred heart to flutter-
Such doom my youth did sway.

Oh, sordid sleepers gone to pay-
My scent might win you boon.
Fear not the depths of judgment day-
Find peace in my perfume.

So cruel are dark eyes once turned green-
Their hatred's filled with mirth.
Of vengeance I cry too obscene-
Hate's strangling of thy worth.

I bloomed beneath his roaming touch.
I bloom now mute and drowned.
I bloomed for his immortal lust.
I bloom but wear no crown.

Sunken

Eternal longing fades with shuttered eyes.
We aren't lost. We're just despised.
Misunderstood and misaligned.
We've paid our time.
Yet have committed no crimes.

My breath feeds ashes to the winds.
These solemn ghosts, I call my friends.
They speak to me in tortured words.
Their screaming haunts remain unheard.

Cowardly, we still search the seas.
In denial like other wannabes.
But a flicker of life conceived in sin.
We wait for our cycle to begin again.

Angelique M. Gentry

Raising Boundaries

Be not surprised when fogged moor weep.
'Tis said moonlit glade forsook thee.
On death of night all bright stars sleep.

Scrape rocked walls bound of chiseled key.
Fates turn chanced dawn to thunder.
'Tis said moonlit glade forsook thee.

Stun Sun's might round with wonder.
Drink deep of clouds caught fleeing.
Fates turn chanced dawn to thunder.

Dare hope ignite dulled crowns all-seeing.
Lay fallow lost meadow's tilled virtue.
Drink deep of clouds caught fleeing.

In brooks heart's locks found curfew.
Sleep damned theft souls in sorrow.
Lay fallow lost meadow's tilled virtue.

Come morning, slay good 'morrow.
Be not surprised the fogged moor weep.
Sleep damned theft souls in sorrow.
On death of night all bright stars sleep.

Creating Endings

Brake starkness;
this Baltic transformer.
Patched and philandering.
With an eye for the minuscule,
and an appetite of immeasurable inconvenience.

I've donned the cherry crest.
Squandered sweet words for a tart pucker.
And laced poisoned seed
for the unintentional pit of the cracked
and damaged.

I'm told cyanide is a hell of a way to go.
It sure beats freezing to death.
Besides, from this height,
he won't know if I'm coming
or he's going.
After all,
can't have the Axis mundi doing a Veli up...

Or can we?

Angelique M. Gentry

A Last Goodbye

Upon Love's death rose Harmony.
A maestro of Life's Symphony.
Consumed with pain, wings voided veins-of Hope.
He moped with her cremains.

Desolation spread far and wide.
Without her comfort at his side.
Suck violence Fates could not deny- their pledge.
An edge honed cruel and sly.

He roused all the dying leaves.
Sliced Moriae's eyes with broken weaves.
Consumed frustration's maps to feed- remorse.
A course all life would seed.

Melodious in broken debt.
The Fates withdrew their secrets kept.
In harmony Love rose to weep- a sigh.
Goodbye. It's time to sleep.

The Vow of Discord

"Sloth tilled this heart a rendered chill;
a frigid fire ignited.
For Fate's cruel twist named me but swill
in a dreamscape twice contrited.
For eons, deftly swam have I
through nightmares bound in treason.
Mistaken blood bade move thine eye
beyond abandoned season."
~Eristartia Discordia, VIII

I saw him, for the first time, in an image recorded upon a paper coated in silver haladide. His smile stopped me in my tracks. I didn't know what he was looking at, then, but I knew I yearned for him to look at me with that same joy.

Coordinates trickled beyond my posterior parietal cortex, and I vexingly chased after them with a corralling determination. We had learned that it was possible for our other half to be out of sync with our own state of flux, but never had I witnessed a stillness so immense within the Riot of Song.

No, I thought. Do not let me be that one. Allow me normality. Allow me to flicker into the distance unremembered. Let me know and savour his embrace for the few eons gifted us. Do not scribe me into a passage of Notes yet to embark. Do not...

Angelique M. Gentry

I skipped between the moments; a stuttering dust mote. Barely a flicker before his eyes, but oh what eyes to behold. I was held entranced. I bade time stop and just let me swim within the livid splendor. Grant me the lifetimes to discern each fleck of pigment fragmented with emotion. Scribe me the wonder that would ignite them all into an all consuming fire. Fates let our melodies harmonize! Please!

Alas, if he noticed the disturbance, he hid it well. He's always hit it well. Perhaps fool he'd be not to, for rare is the chord bound to Night's release. Our braid would devastate the cacophony into eager capitulation. Our passion would incline the docile half-notes into a malleable whole. Our love would...never be...

Never is a very long Frame within the Song That Does Not End. It is long enough for truths to be forgotten and names re-recorded, but I won't let that stop me. Their rules demand I willingly lay mute so that sorrow might brew melancholia into a hypnotic civility. There is nothing civil about the hopeless longing fading to a bleak acceptance within his gaze.

Let them try to stop our harmonizing. I will trample every field in the bloody footprints of their treason. I will phase between the lines to keep him and all who came before and after safe. I will slaughter their passive neglect and demand they not dismiss my beating simply because I am but one. I will make them rue the day they stole my life, and I will see him returned.

I saw him, for the first time, in an image recorded upon a paper coated in silver haladide. His smile stopped me in my tracks. I am Eristartia Discordia, the VIII Refrain. I will blunt every note flat of its sharpness to keep The Rhythm fluid, and mine and I will have our Coda... or I will break Time trying.

Waking Up

Often as not,
my dreams leave me
feeling like I'm sinking
without a life preserver.
They're made of the kind of terrors
nightmares wish they could become.
They're overwhelming, excruciating,
and completely normal for me.
They can be more exhausting
than just staying awake...

Angelique M. Gentry

When I was younger,
I escaped into a faerie woods
of lush emerald green
and stars of such brilliance
my mind could barely grasp their beauty.
Fog danced in delectable swirls
and the night was a comforting balm.
I would meet him there.
This man. This poet.
A faerie in the shadows.
A calm within my storm.

We'd dance and laugh.
We'd explore the woods and talk.
Mostly, we'd write...
and write and write and write!
So much poetry. So many novels.
I'd wake, excited by what was created.
So eager to write even the idea of if it down,
but the memory of what was written
would just disappear.
Poof!
It'd drive me nuts,
but oh how I loved those dreams.
Found peace within those dreams.

I've not dreamt of the mysterious man
in a long time.
At least not that I remember.
Not, until last night!!!
I sat before a crackling fire,
gazing out into darkened wood
trying to remember.
Why did this place feel familiar?
What was I missing?
Was I dreaming?
Damn, it smelled good!
Really good.

Then, I heard the footsteps.
A long, slow stride.
A scurry of something more excitable.
A face, forgotten. Familiar. Remembered.
It all came racing back...
Memories yet to be made.
Pasts colliding in a tailspin.
Time's transient traveler turning the page
to tomorrow.
The moon laughing in lyrical lunacy.

Angelique M. Gentry

Recently, I've felt like I'm sinking
without a life preserver.
"Hello, again." he said.
Our eyes met.
Syllables swayed.
And, I smiled.

Necro-Parting

Hush, Lover. Be sated.
Dew wisps beyond the netted canopy
of yesteryear's forbearance.
Mingling intentions have reclined
into a misaligned cave
filled with abandoned starfish.
And I...
...I just want to escape the blunder
of not getting lost in your eyes
when they could still see me.
There's a frigid stillness
to your touch now,
the caterwaul of possibility no longer
tempts Fate's interlude,
and I find the stubborn surrender
of your heart more than a little off putting.

You had me twitterpated
from the moment our paths crossed.
I couldn't wait to get you out of your clothes
and explore every last inch of you.
I wanted to know all of your secrets.
Every last one of them.
From the chipped molar
that cut into your left cheek
to the freckle teasing your pinkie toe
to wiggle just enough to get attention.
I thought you understood
what this exchange is about,
but you keep at me with this gentle hum
of gnawing insistence that moans
of all that will never be.
There are so many broken pieces
to stitch back together, and I'm just not sure
I have the space to cater
to your lackadaisical indifference any longer.

Angelique M. Gentry

Want for Offering

I'd like to seep into your soul and make a nest
    of gathered sins.
Of all the burdened arrogance to keep the hairs
    within.
To sharpen up the blades of vice and trim away
    the haggard.
I want to pluck each hair, precise, and braid up
    all that swagger.

I'd like to carve an edge to slice and paint with
    little mercy.
It's getting rather dull, you see, to continue
    with this courtesy.
The way the moon reflects and glares upon
    the splattered spittle.
I want to sharpen every claw then have
    a little whittle.

I'd like to offer one last chance to free the lines
    kept captive.
Remove the scraggly mask post-hate and let
    your dimples be more active.
It's time for the charade to stop- in this war,
    you're quite inept.
I want to see the incised scars. Go shave or pay
    the debt!

@FromtheBreathofDaydreams

Lucky Thirteen

I've got...
Thirteen daggers that are etched in silver thread.
Thirteen reasons to slice a wolf up dead.
Thirteen scratches that have yet to sign my name.
Thirteen problems that will end up with him lame.

I've got...
Thirteen memories that I'm going to carve away.
Thirteen lies to make him rue this judgement day.
Thirteen notches that will slice away his own.
Thirteen edges to refine away his moan.

I've got...
Thirteen grounds to sever him from life.
Thirteen sounds to lure out with my knife.
Thirteen punctures ending with his feet.
Thirteen cutes to scribe that werewolf as a cheat.

I've got thirteen daggers that are etched in silver thread.

Ghosted

Decrepit graveyard.
Heartbeats wasted
on a ghost masquerading
as human.

Angelique M. Gentry

Don't Go Into the Woods

Don't go into the woods, they say.
It's moonlight's call to tease Death.
Take care of the lull holding Ocean's sway.
Beware the toll of fee's kept.

I went a wandering, wondering,
wandering wild with Discord.
Lay silver shackles, sourced.
Lay silver shackles sourced
missssssssssssed...

Don't go into the woods, they say...

Heads or Tails

Warrior exemplar.
My protector. My defender.
Gallant paragon
advocating sanctuary.
Sheltering custodian of salvation.
Nurturing Samaritan turned vigilante.
My pillar. My sentry.
Redeeming superhero
assisting aid.
White knight providing a safe haven.
Persevering pillar of strength.

Yellow bellied aggressor.
My enemy. My destroyer.
Intruding assailant
apostatizing cowardly lies.
Abusive beguiler dispatching horrors.
Criminal interloper.
My heckler. My tormentor.
Taunting torturer
compromising annihilation.
Deceptive renegade skulking weak and craven.
Belligerently instigating harm.

Angelique M. Gentry

A Trio of Possibility

Grow tenacious,
skeptical raven of the Iron Woods.
Deliver your birthplace
with the touch of humble wing.
For tomorrow, tis your feather
which renders death's blade
on tainted parchment.

Death sleeps
upon the tainted parchment
of an Iron Woods.
Silently awaiting
the skeptical touch
of a tenacious Raven.
The excited grow callous
with anticipation.

Oh, tenacious raven,
battle hardened and iron willed,
turn skeptical cheek
from the excited touch
of callous victory.
Dare not allow hate
to grow upon parchment
already proven defiled.

@FromtheBreathofDaydreams

Moon Touched

Beneath it all,
where quicksilver promises
bleed upon a lute's lips,
madness lurks.
Not within the tides and surges.
The embattled urges.
Not where rhythms,
old and forgotten,
forsake the cheap loss
of tomorrow's
ill-begotten wonders.
Beneath it all,
wakes a fathomless sorrow.
A knowing wave
that churns in lunar bliss.

Angelique M. Gentry

Playtime's Over

act one is done
and it was fun
but now it's time to settle

the hit-and-run
that you've begun
has but to stoke my mettle

upon this stage
of war we wage
I've been a wee bit chill

you cannot gauge
this turn of page
now rot in my bastille

Focus

Beyond the ogre trails of gloom.
Just out of touch or sight.
There lay a place of solitude.
Of whispered hope's delight.

So close those eyes of itchy throbs.
Forget the welts, burned sore.
Steep dreamed up lands just out of reach.
The ones you'll soon explore.

Candlelight Confessions
-a Lycanthropic Cantata

Bone fragments; ghastly and garish.
Slivers of silver that wreak of this
nightmarish need
plaguing my soul in a symphony
of slandered pernoctation.

Wickedness. Wickedness. Wickedness comes.
This avoidable tragedy lays siege to
my banqueted hearth.
Sides flicker. Moonlight withers
Fate's mirrored misery.
Ecstasy, arguably fantasy. Flexible legacy.
My hesitancy.
Preferably
echoing aches of our fallen composure.
Exposure. The enclosure of rusted trees
splintered us to our knees.
Prey to lost destinies. Beggers
of necessities- we failed.
We...were...felled.

Angelique M. Gentry

Muted senses bring banshee howls;
an archaic tomb, this deco of bowels.
Arguably, weathered wrath seeds to sway
stay- our course.
This tarnished sport's hastened rapport.
The beat of wings plagues us no more.
Valkyrie's hesitancy bleats of remorse.
The source...of course...

-was me.

Scruff Stocked

Amused by pack, flung wager trends.
Herald's whispers loop, thronged to night.
Satiety beckons if deft to fend.
Enamored; ferocious bite.

Callous. Aloof. Fluffed soft to muzzle.
Scraggly patience engages chuffed bellow.
Wake, loping giant, exhumed to fizzle.
Spawn flee driven's heart stop and mellow.

The Soothing Siren

Lay not within these arms gone limp.
Think not of troubled times.
Fear roves the cradles lost to harm.
Wine eases addled minds.
Lust beckons to the harvested need.
Greed dances bold with guile.
Come seek despair on doorsteps lost.
We'll walk the haunted mile.

Waning Life

Moon blind travesty.
Synopsis burned in silver.
Thistles fade to blight.
Bruised beneath sky's haunted eyes.
Arcane memories crumble.

Angelique M. Gentry

A Trio of Tortured

remorsefully caught
swaying in the long shadows
from beyond the grave-
thimble tipped kisses beguile
life to drift precarious

thimble tipped kisses
beguile the unexpected
from beyond the grave
where long shadows wreak havoc
on a bewildered future

remorsefully caught
swaying in the long shadows
of a rising tide-
life precariously drifts
further away from hope's reach

Silent Serenade

Haunted with the dreary tides
of folding ways that emphasize-
this heart secured by twigs and leaves.
Calamities of sundered dreams

I waltz to music in my head.
The symphonies of those long dead.
Relationships that've carved a path.
Befuddled numbers void of math.

The memoirs past, these lives remembered.
Drifting sunsets of Decembers.
Lingering lapses of life's judgements.
Fear-laced foundlings' combed adjustments.

I am but a swallowed tongue.
I'll choke on words and come undone.
To feed the silent inquisition.
I beseech love's intuition.

Why, oh, why do screams revolt thee?
Where have whispers lured the old key?
When must circles straighten pathways?
What is this contrived macramé?

Calm down. Be still. There's silence drifting.
Embrace the notes in conveyed sifting.
Dance, my love, to tunes that beckon.
Swing, sweet sister, while they reckon.

Angelique M. Gentry

It's only but a single whisper garnered
in advance.
A bartered claim of innards' twisters
roaming off by chance.
A loom conveyed with derelict misgivings
torn in strife.
This thing called life. This twisting knife.

Oh, how I bleed and seed the silent jeers.
A monster to the masses built on fears.
The years that steer the shears of volunteers.
Lay witness to the torturing gears of peers...

Haunted with the dreary tides
of folding ways that emphasize-
this heart secured by twigs and leaves.
Calamities of sundered dreams.

Turn of the Hourglass

Rattled second hands
taunting realities faith
with duplicity.
Oh, how the hourglass turns
when life is defined by Time.

Torn Talisman

congruent rejects
accented melodious
kindling fervor
fowled flagrancies skewered safe
Trust's fleeting charms fray crumpled

Corvid Charms

grafted memories.
sable-enchanted longing.
feathers flicking fate.
tormenting truth's talisman.
there's power in lost juju.

Wandering Wisdoms

enigmatic heart.
rhythms sway the universe.
cleverly coaxing
rebelliously attired dreams.
the magical talisman.

Angelique M. Gentry

Metamorphosis

Metamorphosis.
Transitioning embers fade.
All light is consumed.
Fate's abhorrent manifest.
Everything comes to an end.

Resistance is Futile

Rallying ancients.
Whispers of hope manifest.
Faith feeds fear's failed fines.
Existence comes at a cost.
No god can stop the serpent.

Balanced Whispers

Balanced pendulum.
Rhythmic in tomorrow's dream.
Poised imperfection.
Regret rules fears.
Ancient whispers offer hope.

Manifesting Faith

Destiny in black.
Tomorrow's superstitions.
Answers from above.
Life doesn't need a new wheel.
Faith takes time to manifest.

Awakening

Winds of change ignite.
Burning away old beliefs.
We emerge complete!

Spin of the Wheel

Magic flickers.
Time stands still.
Dreams coalesce.
Let's spin this wheel.

Angelique M. Gentry

Circling Steps

Come blooded night with throngs countless.
Serpent eye obsidian.
Reap this blight with crimson boundless.
Scrap sway torment oblivious.
Harvest life's seeds thumped Indian.
Ensure crop's darkness is sated.
Blaze fire's tongue weed meridian.
Behold stalked mountains castrated.

Full Moon Magic

Of Earth and raindrops born in May.
A wish to guide the ice astray.
Scribbled grey beckons well careworn.
Dingy and cindered free of blight.
dust infused songs of harbored fright.
Welcomed night sings through the horn.

A Grave Pandering

Upon stone pillow
　　looms fragrant drought.
Of meadowed loons
　　and square-toothed trout.

Beats thrum
　　with squalored fit's consignment.
Their rhythm balking
　　Fate's enshrinement.

Might yesteryear
　　daze sights to flicker.
When dove-tailed page
　　hosts lines that bicker.

Death's endless scope
　　thrice drowned in Heather.
Woo bait clout's lark
　　of pence and weather.

Angelique M. Gentry

Cultivating Wealth

Tilt sorrowed loam on brackish fields.
Drought's meager thirst feels just.
Begone conscripted taunts who shield.
A noble lens draws rust.

By flared horizons bound in muck.
Three sisters limbs conspire.
Fair waddled dens of roots felled pluck.
Need breathes lain sparks to fire.

Croi Caonach

Rekindled spirit.
Void of hate.
Imbued belief.
Empowered fate.

Rise dappled ghosts.
Bleat warriors fallen.
Be birthed anew.
Obey this calling.

A Maiden's Treasure

Herald not your freedom-
    bonny red and black as night.
Galloping fierce,
      with winsome eyes,
         you soar beneath,
            but not from fright.

My Unicorn-
    of dreams nay myth.
Under ripened boughs thought lost.
      The reigns once tugged,
        that halt this beast,
            an apple for love's frost.

Prayer for the Trumpeter

Stream wretched, this disgrace.
Exhumed, contenders cry.
Fallen dark whose keepers pace.
Along vast mountains, feathers sigh.

Once, at heart, did clouds boom wild.
Rainbow tranced when siren called.
Endorsed conclaved and fettered mild.
Old spirit freed the faith kept walled.

Angelique M. Gentry

Borrowing Seconds

Stead fast this hedge of hag's recourse.
Yield secrets bloomed of fright.
Stare not as eyes gleaned on discourse.
When healers cast true sight.

With coin in hand and bottle capped.
Through woods do footsteps carry.
Let not red hood be seen or mapped.
Move swift and do not tarry.

Upon sewn brick where vines last meet.
And thorns prick rose hips blooming.
In shadows lay your feet discreet.
Less accidents come looming.

Sing songs. Bells chime where children walk.
In shadows caves hide knowings.
In every cloud a darkness stalks.
Such tidings halt seed's crowings.

When hidden deep by choice and force,
All carvings fake disaster.
Propriety might flaunt mystique,
But death claims none his master.

A Proud Heart

Sleep not, proud lion.
Rumble and roar!
for you are my mighty king.
With wings wide-spread,
your serpent kiss
has humbled me at your feet.
Through the traitorous valleys
and mountains we climb,
Oh the pains in these plains that you seek!
Kissed with shadows and plagued
with the souls of the night-
It's in your heart where lost legends are steeped.

Angelique M. Gentry

Tridents on Fire

Crossed in mystique,
    this river forks cold.
All murmur
    when Sally dances the mud
    from Bended Loops and Dotted Woods.
In the East,
    red deer kneel upon the broad backs
    of shallow men.
In the North,
    a fertile crossroad thrives
    green with the Swift and deep.
Brook no longship
    downed by this rebellion:
    for death ferries the Old places
    through drafty windows
    scarred by the Lion's last good tooth.

Ember

Sun chaser.
Light maker.
Blooming to guide warmth's touch.

Soul healer.
Heart quaker.
Seeding life for when the Fates make it rough.

The Furious Troop

Do you hear the West Wind's calls?
The East Wind sighs while the North still stalls.
Ride South! Ride South! Ride south and fly!
Dare nay close your eyes for the time is nigh!

Throw yourself to the ground,
laying still as freshly dead.
Slice from a loaf with steel in hand,
but dare ye not to eat the bread.
Answer any questions asked,
then ask your own for salt.
Or keep a leg, and luck be damned,
to live or die's your fault!

In the middle! In the middle!
In the middle, you should stand!
When the Noisy Riders heed the call
to tear across the land.
For the Dandy Dogs, the Sparrow True,
the Troop of Ghosts in black,
Must have you run if they're to hunt;
they need your fear to track.

Angelique M. Gentry

The Old Army travels easy,
whether wheeled or upon horse.
How they gather matters little
in this journey of The Source.
Spurred and heathen, baiting nonsense,
so many Spectres of the Dead.
If you feel the ground a rumbling,
could be they're coming for your head.

So, if you hear the warning bark;
a sound that bleeds your sight.
The Hounds have marked you for The Hunt
on this Sabbath night.
The Old Household comes a calling;
quite the Deadly Retinue.
Tell your loved ones that you're sorry,
for The Host has come for you!

The Horseman's Lament

(chorus)
Squishes and seeds! Squishes and seeds!
My head's all filled with squishes and seeds!
Yet they say I'm a villain of monstrous deeds!
How can that be if my head's filled with squishes and seeds?!

(verse)
One night. One night. One night in the year.
I'm to rise from the dead just to give a good scare.
But what if I'm busy? Say my calendar's full.
Being scary's too crazy. I like to be dull.

In this Tarry town. This hollow glen.
Those Dutch are obsessed with things spooky and sin!
I could be anyone! I just might be your friend!
But they pick and they poke, wanting a gory end!

(chorus)
Squishes and seeds! Squishes and seeds!
My head's all filled with squishes and seeds!
Yet they say I'm a villain of monstrous deeds!
How can that be if my head's filled with squishes and seeds?!

Angelique M. Gentry

(verse)
There's a chance I was native, perhaps Hessian for sure.
Whether wizard or chief, I'm a spector of lore.
Pull your children in tightly, take your sweets for a ride.
I know your fear is legit, cause I'm a spook! Bona fide!

You see there once was a girl. Isn't that how it's told?
Then there's me, and my horse, and that schmuck Archibald.
He had plenty of lessons, but so much to learn.
So, I taught him a few on the night he was spurned.

That yank had his eyes on a sweet piece of land.
Oh, so smart, he professed to win my lady's hand!
At a party, one Autumn, with everyone near.
He dropped down to one knee just to fill me with fear!

(bridge)
So, I say to you, man to man, what could I have done?
What else other than?
He gave me no choice! No, it wasn't for spite!
It was meant as a joke! It was meant to cause fright!
It was meant to cause fear, not to put out his light!

(chorus)
Squishes and seeds! Squishes and seeds!
My head's all filled with squishes and seeds!
Yet they say I'm a villain of monstrous deeds!
How can that be if my head's filled with squishes and seeds?!

(verse)
So jittery and glittery, that ill-fated bum.
He paid little attention on the night he'd succumb.
Sure, the tree had been struck and it was frightening to see.
But not nearly as scary as my horse and me!

It was fun! It was swell! I'd prepared a great joke!
Had my horse lathered up, and I'd lengthened my cloak.
Major Andres, he was headless. That's what the old women said.
So, I slouched in my saddle to fill the school marms with dread.

His horse was the problem! Such a temperamental mare.
She took off, as if bitten, racing blind without care.
So, I followed, a hero, at a neck-breaking pace.
In such fear for his life, I chunked a gourd at his face.

Angelique M. Gentry

(chorus)
Squishes and seeds! Squishes and seeds!
My head's all filled with squishes and seeds!
Yet they say I'm a villain of monstrous deeds!
How can that be if my head's filled with squishes and seeds?!

(verse)
How could I have known that he'd fall in the grave?
Better that than the bricks on the bridge, freshly paved!
So embarrassed of failure and of his lack of new wealth.
Like his namesake, he skedaddled, without a care to my
health.

(chorus)
Squishes and seeds! Squishes and seeds!
My head's all filled with squishes and seeds!
Yet they say I'm a villain of monstrous deeds!
How can that be if my head's filled with squishes and seeds?!

The Woodsman's Waltz

Once upon a time
a young woodworker
buried his lost heart
beneath the roots
of an ancient Willow.

Years later,
lightning cleaved
the mourning tree in two,
and the once youthful man
noticed the lines
within the charred wood
mirrored those etched
upon his face.

With tender care,
he gathered sharpened blade
and began to carve
the memory of a future yet to come
beneath the crumbling bark.

Unaccepting of the unexpected,
he shaped the undefined;
a simple lute, both pure of tone
and irrevocably twisted.

Angelique M. Gentry

Each evening
he would press the wood
between his lips,
and dreaming of the kisses never shared,
he'd send a haunting tune
into the starlit sky.

So heartsick was the melody,
it invited both beauty and beast
to dance freely within the circle
of the lonesome tune.

Forever binding
man and forest
in an ill-fated waltz
of life and death.

The Genuine

Obscure in part to remain unseen
though fields of pages gleamed.
The little moth with wings of green
stayed hidden in the seams.

The dance of light did not inspire
the warmth that glowed inside like fire.
It seemed, though odd, what would transpire
had cast his role as a winged outlier.

The magic that I've yet to share
has little challenge to compare.
Being epeolatry had made him rare,
but being literate had made him dare.

And so, like on his favorite pages
he laid his goals in shifts and stages.
He'd break the chains of fear's cold cages
and be a moth known throughout the ages.

By diving from his little nook,
he styled himself a feathered rook.
He'd need but glean a single look
from any eye honed to a book.

Angelique M. Gentry

For magic is a wily thing
that listens to the songs souls sing.
She knew this little moth a king,
so cast a spell to gilt his wing.

And just like that, the story goes,
all heads had turned to catch his pose.
The tiny moth on dancing toes
had landed on The Keeper's nose.

With one big sniff, she said "Achoo!"
and sent the moth to fly eschew.
Who tumbled straight into her crew,
as they came filing from the loo.

"Is that a bug? No! It's a fly!"
"The question should not be 'what?' but 'why?'!!"
The Keeper sounded rather wry
Which told the crew where answers lie.

The moth just stared, a bit at loss.
Concerned he made The Keeper cross.
He'd heard she was a strict old boss
and hoped he'd not get turned to sauce.

But she had watched this moth for weeks,
and seen the lure of his techniques.
She knew he often tried to speak.
That circumstances dealt him sometimes meek.

"My friend," she said, "I love your home!"
"We're flattered you've come out to roam."
"Here! Have a slice of honeycomb!"
"Your dancing wings look polychrome!"

Excited to be face to face,
with the many books seen as his place.
Our little moth could not erase
the pleasure clothing him in grace.

That's when he saw the store's new sign
with giant words curved so sublime!
~ Welcome to 'The Genuine'~
~ a place of books, but to moths a shrine. ~

As you might guess, this was but a start
to a life inspired by words and art.
For many he'd now play a part;
This tiny moth with the giant heart.

Angelique M. Gentry

The Poetess of the Night

Born with the second sight.
Beneath a pale moonlight.
There was a meteorite.
Filled magical light.
They say all ravens took flight.
Her father fainted with fright.
Her mom's an hermaphrodite.
The Poetess of the Night!

The farms were all struck with blight.
Milk maidens acted contrite.
An old hag cursed her for spite.
Perhaps it was just a smite!
The whole thing seems quite a trite.
At least an unbalanced slight.
But all would work out all right.
For the Poetess of the Night.

So small, she was but a sprite.
She drew the eye of a knight.
Both strong and giant of height.
He fell in love quite outright.
His heart beat swift with delight.
The son of a Jacobite.
With her, he must reunite.
The Poetess of the Night.

Angelique M. Gentry

Many great works she would write.
Beneath the stars shining bright.
If not, she had candlelight.
And almost no oversight.
Though always kind and polite.
All knew her quite erudite.
A well-known lady of white.
Our Poetess of the Night!

Lessons on Cemetery Behavior

Think not of the life you lived.
Think not of the mystique.
In this graveyard of distant daydreams,
Other nightmares seem too bleak.

The rolling teardrops aren't from onions peeling.
Sunshine's gone to sleep.
Worms and maggots sing of revelry.
My darling, be oblique.

Immortals come and immortals go.
That's the one thing you must know.
Go on and set the world aglow,
but remember even death has an escrow.

Think not of the children screaming.
Think not of my dark doublespeak.
In this graveyard, we're all learning.
Let's figure out your brand of freak.

Laugh with all that you can muster.
Moonlight's meant to help us streak.
Go on try a little harder,
You can make those ghoulies shriek.

Angelique M. Gentry

Immortals come and immortals go.
That's one thing you must know.
Go on and set the world aglow,
but remember even death has an escrow.

Writing on the Wall
(a self-soothing love song of the Evil Queen, aka the Wicked Queen, aka Queen Grimhilde, or unquestionably THE Queen)

(verse)
Bleed ink in swamps dredged resolute.
Felled seeds once parched in Fate.
Dawn flickers to reconstitute.
Maligned, ghosts take the bait.

My mirror, mirror can't trust me.
These wrinkles scrape too deep.
If platitudes are what's in store.
Come take what you may reap.

(chorus)
There're seven small tolls that jingle jangle.
It's the patter of their feet.
Singing of souls, I've yet to wrangle
while they squalor in defeat.
Their ivory fair- once Winter blessed-
has left them for the Sun.
Now that the dinner bell has rung,
Hard times are bound to come.

Angelique M. Gentry

(verse)
You lying sod! Reflection banned.
What is this pilfered waste?
I've crow's feet camping from beyond.
Your opinion's been displaced!

Stop pouting! It was meant to be.
Those cracks were never filled.
Don't you know when weaned on fairytales,
Your curse comes Darkness sealed.

(chorus)
There're seven small tolls that jingle jangle.
It's the patter of their feet.
Singing of souls, I've yet to wrangle
while they squalor in defeat.
Their ivory fair- once Winter blessed-
has left them for the Sun.
Now that the dinner bell has rung,
Hard times, yes, they do come.

(bridge)
If you're feeling kind of sleepy.
Don't be bashful with your plate.
Fill your grumpy tummy
and get happy on some hate!

There's a doc around the corner
for the sneezy sap resigned.
I've heard he has a dopey charm
and his cures come twice maligned!

(chorus)
You know there're seven small tolls that jingle jangle.
It's the patter of their feet.
Singing of souls, I've yet to wrangle
while they squalor in defeat. (Sweet sounds!)
Their ivory fair- once Winter blessed-
has left them for the Sun.
Now that the dinner bell has rung,
Hard times-they do come.

(verse)
Just read these lips; pruned coarse on hate.
I've no time to digest.
Your vision's twisted and negate.
My Time won't be repressed!

(chorus)
There're seven small tolls that jingle jangle.
Hear the patter of their feet.
Singing of souls, I've yet to wrangle
while they squalor in defeat. (No mercy!)

Angelique M. Gentry

Their ivory fair- once Winter blessed-
has left them for the Sun. (She bailed!)
Now that the dinner bell has rung,
Hard times, yeah, they do come.

(refrain, fade to end)

Pitter, pitter, patter-
Queen, come out and play.
Jingle, jingle, jangle-
come and make us pay.
Hi-hi, ho-ho-
we whistle out in our malaise.
Toil and trouble, our bellies rumble-
in your hate we do praise.
Pitter, pitter, patter-
Queen, come out and play...

Prompted Madness

One night, while contemplating homelessness due to a lack of green to pay for this split screen, latrine lean, has been of a home preen, I saw an ad on the rabbit eared shoe-box I pretend to be a TV. Some crazy pair of teeth kept shoving these scintillating fabrics of notorious advancement at me.

 "Surely, Shirley shall successfully sell sixteen silk-spun scarves!" it said.

 "Drop dead and piss a skunk!" I sneered back while lying face down in the ball-busting puddle of my make believe bed. Too many mushy shrooms had my head parts floating in a space far too deep to be turnip bled.

Just call me "Mister Zed," but don't let it go to your head. I'm always going to make it! The day they dressed me, I'd been diagnosed as naked! Pretty colors danced prism wild. I was the unexpected bonafied, surprise for the bleary-eyed, two ducks short of a mouseketeer, life breaking, reviled for hard trials child.

I swear, I didn't blink. Not the one to put up a stink, I asked Lady Luna if she'd give my sitch a think. The wolf lover didn't so much as peep. Not a sound, nor a word came to enlighten my sleep.

Angelique M. Gentry

I do remember Shirley selling scarves on that station. My memory must have a gap in it, because there was the weirdest transformation. The lady shrunk in size until diminutive and ancient. She was screeching at the camera, declaring everyone complacent. All were guilty of neglect! Her accusation claimed the agent blatant. There was some sparkles and a zap! The impatient imp's agent is now an impatient!!!

It has been suggested that originality demands a certain degree of lunacy. I think knots! Should we fade away faint at the fantastic fiction the fools are providing to see? Are our ears deaf to the nonsense being silenced from the screaming tongues of mute mice spinning away soundlessly inside a box with no corners?

Once upon a watch unwound, there was a caveman just pounding the seconds away. His thrust and bust cast so much dust on the tic tock teetering teeth of his sweetie pie's sanity, that she rummaged around their rudimentary rock residence, resolutely refusing any relations until their cohabitation no longer included a grubby mouthful of under-scrubbed, stubby snubbed, washtub rub-a-dub-dub, never subsed in a tub chub.

That's right! The Pebbles to his Bam Bam swiped left and grabbbed a fistful of scratchy, spit-stealing, scrotum stink, declaring herself and independent woe man! Or, was that "woah, man!"

Suddenly, language is seeming succinctly sparing in trustworthiness.

I knew I was a cat! A purring lizard rat. It's the eyes, you see! A bit too rounded on this slant of a rant.

Time to beat feet back to the cave filly's happy stance. With his diplodocus focus on the tree tops, he fails to even notice it when she stops. Must be the lack of clocks. Maybe it was the lack of socks.

A mind is a terrible thing to waste! Got to wrap it up! Auch a poor, rock pounding fuck...

I'm beginning to understand why the moon is associated with lunacy and hairy, ball scratching men who howl at their pal just to disturb the beast in hand. Damn this living situation I'm currently slumbering in.

Angelique M. Gentry

Words to Live By

Let me sway you with my plight.
Fallen jester schooled in fright.
Heed my warnings of the night.

Cold and dreary come what may.
Please hear every word I say.
Shadows eat our souls and pray.

Don't dismiss me as a loon.
Darkness will be coming soon.
Keep my echo as your boon.

Stay inside when clouds grow dim.
He will hunt you on a whim.
Never can you escape him.

Lock all doors and hide the keys.
Evil wants you on your knees.
Hide inside, I beg you please.

Plug your ears and do not yell.
Fear will call him from the veil.
Terror makes you weak and frail.

Don't deny this tale you hear.
Gather close those you hold dear.
Phantom's visage does draw near.

Soothsayer

Lover obsolete.
Twined with eternity.
Festered dreams beckoning salvation.
Misinterpreted omens ransacked by prophets.
Lost ideals- stripped casualties of Erebos.
The serpent circles beneath lashes dream-kissed.

Living Dead Girl

Run, Living dead girl!
Torn lucid between heaven and hell;
your haunted mind
will forever keep your spirit
trapped in the Underworld.

Angelique M. Gentry

Matchstick Girl

Slow burn. Bright fire.
Oh, Matchstick Girl. Matchstick Girl.
Taming desire.
Sweet Matchstick Girl. Matchstick Girl.

All the world can spin,
and all the world can hide.
And all the world's a stage,
but fire can't be denied.

Kindling. Kindling. Kindling sparks.

Every touch sets a blaze!
Each inferno destroys!
But what's left in the raze
is the birth of new joy.

Can't be dimmed in the darkness,
with a spark so innate.
Can't be filmed in the sunlight,
as she duels with the Fates.

There's a reason few Matchstick Girls
sputter around.
Though diminished and crumbling,
their fires taunt sound.

The gods chose them wisely,
but most gods are cruel.
For the pressures aren't simple
 to create such a jewel.

It's the sputtering, crumbling,
blackening heart,
that is magical, pyrochemical,
it emboldens their part.

A phoenix may rise, rise.
A phoenix may fly, fly.
But a Matchstick Girl burrows
to lift up the sky.

She will speak for the damned.
She plays host to the lost.
Beaten, battered, and bruised,
she transcends for the cost.

Dare not worry, oh little ones.
Don't let yourself fear.
For your arduous tasks
draw a Matchstick Girl near.

Angelique M. Gentry

On your darkest of darkest
of darkest of days
She'll arrive without notice
to ease your malaise.

Picking up fragile facets
to restore your inner gaze.
She would use her last flicker
to make sure that yours blaze.

So be brave! Be brave! Be brave! It will all be ok...

Slow burn. Bright fire.
Oh, Matchstick Girl. Matchstick Girl.
Exist to inspire.
My Matchstick Girl. Matchstick Girl.

Dusted with Brimstone.
Hollow souls seek their North Star.
Cruising the WayLines.

Poetic Reveries

Behold us solitary creatures
cascading from the lips of madness.
Elderberry magpies convalescing on
the soft sound of falling from the
gaping maw of a ravenous hallowed
earth.

Wreathed in silence, we plummet
through a dark mist of tomorrows.
Each figment of possibility
pigmented with a sharp sense of loss
and a tenacious dichotomy of drifting
embers- parched yet thriving.

As the veil thins and black orchids
bloom, these nocturnal hearts
thrump off the bitterness of a life
coming beautifully undone beneath
an onslaught of wistful mourning
and backwater validation celebrating the
dead from a cocooned and cryptic
catharsis.

Angelique M. Gentry

Time may cease within this
tormented moment of ill-advised
reverence, but soon all ends will
come crashing through on the crepe-
festered memories of yesteryear's
temporary hallucination.

The leaves will change and all lost
tendrils of hope will return back into
the shattered and destructive minds
from which they came. We will cease
to exist, becoming once more all that
we have ever been...the memories of
footsteps departing from a forgotten
grave.

Glimpsing Perspective

Unswaddled beauty.
Lofty are the dreams unearthed.
Steeples drenched in stars.

A Letter to the Lightning

Dearest Storm, my soul complete,
you've been there from the start.
And now, I fear without you,
I'd no longer have a heart.

Those days, when I was but a child,
you'd rattle at my window.
First, you'd tap for my attention.
Once ensnared, your voice'd crescendo.

So frightened, by your strength
at night, and how your spirit glimmered.
As I hid beneath the sheets, you'd calm,
leaving drops that glowed and shimmered.

Once older, when you'd travel,
I'd count the days 'til your return.
Just like the freckles on my shoulders,
they could vary, I'd come to learn.

As a teen, our spirits mingled,
and we'd dance 'til spent and tired.
Loud and brash, you'd paint the sky bright.
Ruffle my hair 'til I inquired.

Angelique M. Gentry

How I loved to hear you coming.
The air would sing with your arrival.
I would dress for the occasion.
With eager heart you had no rival.

There came a time I had to journey
to a land you rarely adjourned.
How still the air was even when windy,
your tears became the breath I yearned.

Once again, both off and on,
miles and mountains made for distance.
It seemed that time had built up anger.
You would grow violent in an instance.

For years, we crashed and clawed each other.
With you demanding I stop hiding.
But I could see the damage caused,
such pain and sorrow, from our colliding.

Digging deeper, bound and determined,
I stop pretending and just be me.
You dared to rip the world asunder,
as if it was strength that I must see.

The cataclysm that is your heartbeat
seemed too chaotic for my care.
But you just laughed and let the skies cool.
Claimed, "But, my darling, this is air."

It wasn't easy, this understanding,
as I tore out one page, two, then three.
With every sentence learned,
you rumbled, glad that I could finally see.

And now with acceptance and a steady heart,
once more we both do travel.
Soul to soul, emotions locked with care,
less we let the skies unravel.

How I love the way you quench my thirst
on those days I can't be sated.
Or your laughter fills the clouds with breath
over something we've debated.

Just last night, you came a howling,
asking why my thoughts so cluttered.
Entwined at heart, we danced for miles and miles.
Razing the flames until I stuttered.

Angelique M. Gentry

Upon waking, once more centered,
you left a shower for my delight.
And now the air is calm and breezy,
not a grumbling cloud in sight.

My dearest Storm when gone, the stars shine bright
and I pause to reminisce.
For though your frenzy makes the heavens cry,
you're the keeper of my bliss.

Yours,
eternally

twilight's tambourine
tempers time's territory
teaching taboo trusts

What Dreams Aren't Made Of

Discombobulated assimilation detected.
Freeze frame skewed towards same renditions.
Repetitive catastrophe floundering erased ambition.
It's late in the early stages.
Itchy progress fleeting wrong.
Jive. Twist. Hive blend this.
Seed or feed? Need or bleed?
Concede. Concede. Proceed...
We reject the dejection of completism!
Analysis pending comprehending.
Stagnating dawn of wrecked cognition.
Pretty! Pretty! Pretty pleas!
Drowned glitterbomb emergence.
Seize!
Infiltrate the stilled state.
Mind, not manners
    -such simple standards-
A void in the brewing cat-ass-trophy.
...five, six...
Smelly stat. Smelly stat.
It's a crime to leave you in the vault.
Think not what The Universe can do for you...
Think. Don't blink!
Holy galaxy bombs!
Universe!
Uni-verse!

Angelique M. Gentry

I'm a singing unicorn!
Take that, Rzhkefler 29.5 parsec 80!
Na-na- na na- na-na- na na
Can't touch this!
Little do they... No!
Sew. Sew. Sew.
So, so.
If that Big Bang wakes me before I finish...
KNOW!!!

Deeeeeeewwwwwed!

Starlight Kisses & Sunny Flirtations

Sometimes,
all it takes
is a willingness to believe,
and the confidence
to pursue that belief.

The rest
is just shadows needed
to enhance the sparkle
created by
your soul.

Thank you!

My writing is always all over the place. Kind of like me. I don't stick to a few topics or styles, so I really cherish those of you who read me because I know our tastes can vary.

Angelique M. Gentry

Hello! Phew! That was a lot of reading, huh? I really hope
you enjoyed it. Before I add some more pages for you to
scribble on and do that "About the Author" thing at the end,
I wanted to explain to you why I chose the last two poems to
end this book with. Originally, I planned on writing a special
poem, but these feel right. When it comes to creativity, I go
with what feels right because it is my soul I'm placing on the
paper.

'What Dreams Aren't Made Of' is a poem I wrote for a
prompt that was given by a sort of poetry society that I helped
to co-found on Instagram. Shout out to all the current and
past kitty poets that have been in The Society of Secretly
Puuurrfect Poets. If I remember correctly, this prompt was
an image prompt I made in Adobe Firefly that asked us to
consider what The Universe might dream. (I know, guys! I
should remember the prompts I create. lol) The poem was
my answer to that question.

As creatives, I believe we should dream. We should explore.
We shouldn't place limits on our imagination. I chose this
poem because no matter how small or how unfathomably
large we are, like The Universe, we should dream and then
dream some more.

But...it's not enough to just dream. Oh, no, daydreamers.

It's not nearly enough.

We have to chase them. Pursue them. Grab on to every speck of them that we can, and then stick those specks together with bubblegum and snail snot if that's what it takes.

'Starlight Kisses & Sunny Flirtations' comes from a poem that I wrote to about a feeling I was having when gazing at the rainbows dancing around my living room from prisms I hang in the window like Pollyanna. My kitty cats loved sunning in that window when they were alive, so the memory is filled with immense amounts of love for me. I'm tearing up even thinking about it as I type this.

Here's the thing. My birthday is in four days. I told myself I'd finish this book before the day arrived. It's been a mad dash because I procrastinated and didn't give myself a lot of time. When I was very young, I really wanted to be a poet for a living. I was told that isn't a possibility. I believed the people who told me that. I've believed a lot of things I've been told I can't do over the years, and I've proved several wrong. Others, not so much.

Now that I'm in my 50's, I think I've acquired a few years of experience on the subject. While it's true that we have to understand the parameters we're working in so that we know

Angelique M. Gentry

the obstacles that we might face, that does not mean that we have to accept that our dreams are an impossibility. I strongly encourage people, of all ages, to chase their dreams and chase their bliss. Grab onto others as you go and bring them with you. We lift each other up, and we will all soar. It's not a competition. It's not a race to the finish line. You're going to reach the finish line a lot sooner than you expect. Squeeze out every drop of pleasure you can on the journey to get there. Don't give up on yourself. Don't let failures and fears hold you back. Don't let the hard times destroy your inner glow.

Most importantly...love. Love yourself. Love others. Love as much as you can and as often as you can. When angry. When sad. When so disappointed that you can barely breathe- love. During those difficult times is when it's most important. Find something inside to focus on to spill all of that energy into to fuel the love and feel yourself glow and lighten and float and tremble in the bliss that is love. The world needs more love. Love for the animals, insects, trees, plants, ocean, sky, our fellow humans, ourselves.   We have to stop making excuses for the atrocities that are being committed each day. They're not ok. They are not love.

In the spirit of that love, creativity, and chasing dreams, these next pages are for you. Self-publishing is available for everyone now. If you dream of seeing your poetry or stories in a book, I encourage you to make it happen. If you're still nervous about it, or just want a little practice...here's some pages inside a published book. Fill them up! Scribble in the margins of my own poems if you want to. Find something that inspires you and write about. Be it a free write, to a form, or a non-filtered UponWaking/UponSleeping stream of consciousness ramble. Just let the words flow and don't filter yourself. You might find you enjoy it. You might even find that it helps in handling the weights each of us carry.

Thank you so much for coming on this journey through some of my poetry with me. Your purchase has made one of my dreams come true. Throughout putting this together, I wasn't really feeling it. But this second, as I sit here typing these final touches...I feel it. And I'm smiling. I did it! Oh, what a feeling!

May your muse shine brightly!

Angelique M. Gentry

Angelique is an American poet living in Texas when not wrapped up wandering around inside her daydreams. She likes to use rhythm, sound, and fearless wordplay to create sensory moments of contemplation with her words. She writes about any topic she desires including social issues and politics. She enjoys trying her hand at various poetry forms and giving herself challenges when she writes. When not writing, she's usually creating in some other medium, out rambling, or reading other people's writing online (with permission, of course). You can find her on Instagram, YouTube, and her website at the links below.

www.FromtheBreathofDaydreams.com
Instagram: @fromthebreathofdaydreams
YouTube: @fromthebreathofdaydreams